# TALKING IN PICTURES

How Snapchat Changed Cameras, Communication, and Communities

# TALKING IN PICTURES

How Snapchat Changed Cameras, Communication, and Communities

Chelsea Peitz

ISBN-13: 9781544262543
ISBN-10: 154426254X

*This book is dedicated to:*

My husband, Brian
*The first time I saw you, I knew.*

My son, Mason
*My best content yet.*

My brother, Baxter
*I should have hired you sooner.*

My Snapfamily
*Inspired.*

*Much love.*

# Table of Contents

*"People wonder why their daughter is taking 10,000 photos a day. What they don't realize is that she isn't preserving images. She's talking."*

- Evan Spiegel, CEO Snap Inc.

# Preface

*This is the true story of an app that may not exist in a year.*

If you're reading this book right now, you're probably thinking one of two things:

1. Yaaaassss! I love Snapchat and I can't wait to learn more about how it's changed communication and social networks.

   *Great! I'll show you the What, Why, and How of Snapchat:*

   - **What**: *Snapchat is NOT social network—so what is it?*
   - **Why**: *Snapchat disrupted social networks and inspired new ways of communication and community building by tapping into our innate need for connection and the psychology of habits.*
   - **How**: *Snapchat is a tool that can help you build a visible and authentic brand with a camera first strategy.*

2. Ummmmm…ok, so you're in the marketing biz, but you're writing a book about an app whose key features have been easily duplicated—the same app whose user base that is being eclipsed by Instagram and Facebook. Aren't you kind of rearranging deck chairs on the Titanic?

*You could be totally right. Snapchat may cease to exist at any time and become just another failed platform like Meerkat, Blab, or Myspace (RIP), but we have to remember the delivery mechanism doesn't matter, it's the lessons we learn from using that mechanism that hold true meaning. Snapchat has a lot to teach us about the value of a singular maniacal focus on consumer experience, and why innovation always wins. That focus—on fulfilling an unexpressed need among users—is the kind of anticipatory savvy that creates disruption and fosters customer loyalty. Essentially, Snapchat made people want to share their lives through a camera, without them even realizing that's what they wanted. These timeless lessons apply to any platform and serve as teachable moments for anyone who is interested in connecting deeply with a tribe.*

*Let's not get wrapped up in the medium, let's focus on the message.*

■　　■　　■

## WHO AM I?

I am a creator first and a marketer second. I've worked in the real estate industry for over 17 years as a Realtor® and then as a Director of Marketing and Director of Social Strategy for a title insurance company. I teach the real estate community how to leverage social media and digital strategies to build a brand. My focus is sharing what I know about social networks and technology from first-hand experience, serving a very specific niche audience. I've held a professional role as a marketing specialist for over 7 years creating content, speaking on stages, and writing blogs and now a book!

The most important thing you should know about me is that I'm not a social media "expert." Companies don't pay me to build their brands or influence others to take action. I don't have humongous follower counts on any platform because my community has been built with intention, one relationship at a time. I didn't "game the system" or "growth hack" in any way, so everything that you read here is straight from personal experience.

I am a practitioner.

Just so we're clear, I'm not a digital native or a Millennial. I'm a Gen X-er and an almost-40-year-old working mom and wife that didn't grow up with Facebook. I only started using Snapchat in May of 2016. Basically, the odds of Snapchat ever becoming my primary social network were pretty slim.

You should also know that I am heavily biased towards Snapchat, so if you're looking for a totally objective assessment of this app, you won't find it here. Yes, there are other amazingly powerful platforms that may be able to help you build a brand faster, connect with more people at scale, or offer better ways to monetize than Snapchat does, but this book isn't a comparison of social networks or why one is better than another. It's an explanation of why Snapchat played a huge part in the evolution of social media, and how it has impacted the way we communicate.

Since I've started using Snapchat, I have used the app every single day. I believe in doing before boo-ing and I won't give my opinion on something that I haven't personally used. I may not be an expert, but as a practitioner and heavy user, I've earned the right to share my opinion, whether you agree with it or not.

I'm a Snapchat devotee, but not for the reasons you might think. Sure, Snapchat is fun and creative and provides me with a relaxed environment where I'm not afraid to be myself, but the real reason I love this app is the because of the community engagement. I'm fascinated by the evolution of social media and technology and how they impact our behaviors and change our expectations. The community of people I've met through Snapchat has directly impacted my life and business, and using this app has improved my ability to communicate succinctly and confidently in front of a camera. What I have gained from using this app is a personal perspective and a clear understanding of what I value in a social network—real relationships.

■    ■    ■

## WHAT THIS BOOK IS AND ISN'T ABOUT

### IT'S ABOUT:

I believe that Snapchat has a bigger lesson to teach us about human nature. Modern communication is now defined by mobile devices that have earned our acceptance and shaped our expectations of screen-to-screen relationships. I'll share my experience of building my personal brand by using Snapchat, how I organically grew a community, and how Snapchat can be used for business. Keep in mind, the core concepts that I share in this book don't apply **ONLY** to Snapchat.

These chapters contain my personal observations and opinions about a social messaging platform that, I feel, brilliantly capitalized on the psychology of communication and our inherent need for human connection. Together, we will explore why and how Snapchat encouraged hundreds of millions of people to share their lives in the moment and talk *through* images not around them. I'll share insights into how Snapchat leveraged psychology to create ingrained and habitual behaviors in its users, and why so many other competitors felt threatened by its uniquely disruptive features. Lastly, I'll share how you can use Snapchat to create a powerful personal brand, provide value to your community, and develop an authentic core message that resonates with your target audience.

Here's what this book will cover:

- Why Snapchat was a game-changer for social platforms and how it changed human behavior our expectations around communication.
- How Snapchat's innovative features disrupted every major social network.
- How Snapchat created a habit-forming product by tapping into our psychology.
- How to create a camera first strategy using real time visual content to share your message, build a visible personal brand, and connect authentically, not only within Snapchat, **but also within every other social platform.**

## IT'S NOT ABOUT

I want to be clear that this book isn't about proving that Snapchat is a superior social network or messaging app. You may have read blogs prognosticating that "everyone" is leaving Snapchat and migrating to other platforms with copycat features. Let me assure you, those bloggers don't have a crystal ball and neither do I. Listen, I get it—I'm very aware of the current shift in social media and the battle between Facebook, Instagram and Snapchat. I've spent a lot of time and effort building a solid community within Snapchat 100 percent organically and hack-free, so the idea that it could all go away tomorrow is a pretty big bummer.

You won't be bombarded by case studies in this book. You won't only find stories about big brands with big budgets advertising on Snapchat with sponsored face Lenses or Geofilters. I've chosen to include quotes and stories from fellow Snapchatters with whom I have personally connected or met, learned from, and been inspired by during my Snapchat adventure. I specifically chose "everyday" people over big brands and well known influencers because I wanted to hear their stories of success and understand the process that they implemented. I wanted these examples to feel attainable to readers. Reading about huge corporations that hire a fully staffed advertising agency and spend seven figures per ad can be highly educational, but applying the same tactics of a multi-million dollar budget as a solopreneur or small business isn't realistic or very relatable. My goal is to introduce you to people who are just like you and me. I've included their Snapchat username in each quote or story so that you can connect with these amazing humans as well.

This book is not about getting you to use Snapchat. It's about helping you understanding how innovation in social media has become an integral part of our human experience. I find it utterly amazing that we have tools in our phones that connect us to anyone, anywhere, and through them we can share our lives without even saying a word.

Regardless of your personal opinions of Snapchat, my hope is that by reading this book, you may consider a different point of view or possibly gain a deeper understanding about how the app impacted social conversation. I want to help you to understand what's happening with social communities and visual communication and how it applies to building a community, how it can improve your marketing, and why our behaviors and expectations have changed.

Now, let's begin.

# Introduction

*"This is a world where you don't have to invest in a printing press, or a satellite, or a sales team in order to distribute your story anymore."*

- GARY VAYNERCHUK, FOUNDER VAYNERMEDIA

## IN REAL LIFE

I wasn't an early adopter of Snapchat.

Social media was evolving quickly and learning how to navigate multiple platform updates was hard enough for me, let alone testing out every new social app that cropped up. I didn't have time learn how to use the latest shiny object, especially one that wasn't intended for my target demographic. Or so I thought. As I realized later on, when you say you don't have time for something, what you're really saying is that you don't see value in it.

I continued to read countless marketing blogs about the Snapchat's exponential growth and its devoted, almost fanatical user base. I knew a couple of co-workers and friends who had downloaded the app, but I still couldn't wrap my head around how to use Snapchat for something other than just wasting time. I admit, I believed all the hype I had heard (mostly from other Gen X-ers) about Snapchat:

- Only narcissistic Millennials use the app to send silly selfies or naughty photos.
- Finding other users is too hard, and it's virtually impossible to grow an audience in a private environment with limited discovery.
- Generating brand awareness is hopeless, unless you are a big brand with tons of money to use for advertising or an already well-known influencer with an enormous following.
- Making content that vanishes after 24 hours is a waste of time.
- Without a lot of analytics or a public advertising platform, there is no way to measure ROI, scale reach or monetize content.

And then, one morning, everything changed.

■   ■   ■

## DAY TRADING ATTENTION

Keurig on, coffee brewing, and YouTube playing was my typical pre-work morning routine. I got my daily dose of marketing education right from my iPhone on the bathroom counter. At the time, my favorite YouTube series was a marketing docu-vlog called *The DailyVee*. Gary Vaynerchuk, four time best-selling author and international marketing guru, was the creator and host, documenting his daily worklife through video. Many of you may already know his brand as a self-proclaimed, "day trader of attention," who focuses on arbitraging… well, every-thing. He's a raw, street smart immigrant-turned-millionaire who made the word HUSTLE a hashtag. He's not everyone's cup of tea, but no one can deny that he knows what works in business and marketing today.

Vaynerchuk said that thanks to the internet and social networks, every one of us, individual or company, was now a brand with a very vis-ible online reputation. Public reviews, star rating systems, and the ever present comment box made it easy for consumers to throw in their two cents about anything. The end user now confirmed whether or not a brand was who they said they were, and often very publically. Brands didn't hold the power anymore, which meant they had to begin rethinking their old strategies and start pivoting with the market.

Often with enthusiastic fist-pounding and finger-pointing, Vaynerchuk ranted that brands could no longer take the easy way out by simply throwing more money behind advertisements. Salesy pitches, banner ads, and generic posts on a feed weren't going to cut it anymore. Now, brands would need to provide value upfront without the expectation of an immediate return, before going in for "the ask."

Gary had been professing the power of Snapchat on the stages of sold out conferences and on his daily vlog since 2013[2]. Snapchat was attracting consumers who valued authenticity because it was difficult to fake your personality on camera 24/7, and the average user couldn't hack their way to the top. You had to be real and tell stories, which wasn't covered in most marketing courses. He urged marketers to start paying Snapchat some serious respect because the app was connecting with a savvy youth culture that would eventually grow up and buy things. The way they consumed information and interacted with brands was radically different from the generations before them—access and apps trained their behaviors, changed expectations, and shifted attention. Capturing their short attention spans and finding ways to engage with this group one-to-one at scale would become a brand's biggest concern. Creating value and grabbing attention was the right formula— doing that with authenticity and intention was the hard part.

Vaynerchuk evangelized raw, real time video as an incredibly powerful brand-building tool because it exposed our authentic human side. Non-fiction content was more interesting than traditional advertising because it was about telling your own story, and that made it relatable. He encouraged every viewer to become a media company that documented the story of their brand through any and all platforms available. Distribution was key, and using social networks was the solution. We now had our very own personal television channels and a broadcast network in our pockets. We could easily share experiences as they happened, and telling stories now had no barrier to entry.

Brands could use Snapchat to connect with consumers through visual, value-based content, because it would provide *context* to their brand message. Including emotion and facial expressions, or even a location-based Geofilter, could amplify your content and layer additional meaning onto a simple image. Showing someone what you did was way more powerful than just telling them about it. We love good stories and we want to follow someone on their journey from start to finish. Snapchat's camera first platform was ideal for social selling because it allowed viewers to share someone's experience as it happened. Gary said that the only thing we could really scale was our own story because it was the truth that with us each and every day. Words on a page or text in a status update didn't come close to the feeling we got when we saw a smile on someone's face. Communicating eye-to-eye (regardless if it was through a screen) created familiarity, relevance, and a sense of intimacy that can create powerful and authentic experiences for both parties. Those who understood the power of connecting through a screen in a human way would succeed.

Snapchat was more about context than just the content.

I was nodding my head, and I remember saying, "But why would I waste my time making content that just disappears?" And then it happened—Gary described the genius of ephemeral content in one simple sentence:

*"Before you tell a story, you have to have somebody's attention"*

**Ding!**

My ears perked up.

Disappearing content mattered because it captured 100% of the viewers' attention. You only had one shot to see it before it was gone, and if you didn't, too bad, so sad. [insert mind-blown meme here] Of course, this made perfect sense to me now. If someone told me that I would have to pass a test but I would only be able to see the answers for a short period of time, you better believe I would pay attention.

I was starting to get it but still wasn't totally sold on Snapchat just yet. "Okay Gary, I'll give you the attention thing, but what about the lack of discovery and limited audience size?" As if on cue, Gary shared his perspective on the true value of a social network. It wasn't about the number of followers someone had, the real value of a community was its depth. A small community of highly engaged users was exponentially more powerful than millions of empty connections. Vanity metrics like follower counts and likes were meaningless unless they resulted in real conversations or conversions. For Vaynerchuk, Snapchat met all of the modern day requirements for a successful social networking platform: the user base was growing, people were engaging at higher than normal rates, and the power of being in the moment was intoxicating. When I heard his explanation, I felt like I was missing out on something big and that maybe I was becoming one of "the olds." I didn't want to be late to the game, so after experiencing some major FOMO, I decided to learn what all the fuss was about.

I downloaded the app, set up my account and immediately found it frustrating. I couldn't figure out the interface and the different screens. It was like going from a PC to a MAC—all the functions were in different places. I just didn't get it. Where was my newsfeed? How did I find my friends? I quickly realized that I was going to have to put in some time and effort to learn something new.

This app was pretty presumptuous.

■ ■ ■

## LEARNING CURVE

In the beginning, using Snapchat was merely an experiment for me. I had already made up my mind before I had even gotten started—this app wasn't going to be for me, but I might learn some things along the way that could inspire a future blog post. Since I'm a bit of an over-achiever, I committed to Snapping every single day for an entire year, partly because I really wanted to say I had given it the old college try, and partly because I wanted to earn the right to call myself a true user of the platform—go big or go home, right?

The app's ecosystem was inconsistent with other social platforms that I had been using. There wasn't an endless stream-of-consciousness flooding down a feed. There were no albums or status updates - nothing that prompted me to share, "what's on your mind." I couldn't search for people, groups or topics, and I had to know a person's exact username or Snapcode (which is basically a scannable QR code) to even find someone's account. There wasn't any way to buy likes or advertise to a targeted audience, and from what I could tell, there wasn't an easy or obvious way to game the system.

I started reading everything I could find online about Snapchat. I downloaded all the ultimate guides and eBooks. Over time through trial and error, I learned how to use the features, the filters, and send messages by voice, text, and video. I read the hack-filled blog articles and watched every YouTube tutorial that promised to up my Snapgame.

*What those articles didn't teach me was how to create an engaged community, develop a valuable and viable personal brand, or how Snapchat was training our behaviors.*

I had no designs of using Snapchat to create friendships; I was merely using this platform as a marketer who was curious about learning a new tool that perhaps I could teach my audience more about. My goal was to learn if it was a viable option to generate leads and create brand awareness. Because of that, I was solely focused on creating a documentable and somewhat rigid content format. I knew that in order to build a recognizable brand, I would need to focus on developing a core message and consistently deliver that message on a daily basis. I wasn't exactly sure how to create a cohesive storyline so I observed the styles and formats of different Snapchat users I followed.

*There's no shame in being inspired by others. I'm not saying you should carbon copy someone's exact content or style, I'm merely suggesting that modeling yourself after someone whom you admire is a very normal starting point. After a while, you'll inevitably fall into your own groove and make your channel uniquely you. The most important thing is that you do it consistently, and then you'll get better.*

I planned on treating the platform as an actual broadcasting channel and created my own weekday Snapshow called *Chelschat: Marketing Snappily Ever After,* where I shared social media and marketing tips, tools, and strategies that would, "help people grow their business and make more money doing what they loved." At first, it wasn't good. I look back at my beginning Stories and I cringe. We all do. I wasn't looking at the camera, I overused filters and wasn't letting my real personality shine through. But I stuck with it and forced myself to host a show every Monday thru Friday, rain or shine, in sickness and in heath.

I didn't share or re-purpose my content to any other channels—I was committed to staying pure to the Snap (Remember, this was an experiment for me, so I approached this platform with a unique set of intentions). Eventually, I learned what worked for my specific audience and how to get comfortable in front of the camera.

I planned out my content every week, storyboarding and tracking topics in a spreadsheet, and diligently collected ideas for the upcoming week's shows. I was afraid I would eventually run out of ideas or new things to say, but I came across a Seth Godin quote that said that no one has ever suffered from "Talker's Block[1]," which basically meant that if we just start writing and stick to it, we will eventually get better. Ideas will pop up and allow you to succeed. For over a year, I never ran out of things to talk about, and I delivered content every day that resonated with my niche audience. I began developing a reputation as an account you watched to learn about social media marketing.

In the beginning, my content was all business and very little, if any, personal stories, but after a while I began injecting my life, family, and personality into my channel, and that seemed to be the magic formula. After all, it was harder NOT to include my family and home life, and I realized that people wanted to watch someone relatable and entertaining and REAL. I discovered that when I wasn't afraid to showcase my quirky sense of humor or make fun of my own flubs and mistakes, my community laughed with me. I started to love my #onetakesnaps and being fallible seemed to become my best asset. As someone whose career was spent delivering formal presentations in front of an audience, this was a complete departure from all my professional training.

I found there was power in being human.

While I was creating content, I was also trying to find more channels to watch because when I downloaded the app, I only knew one other person who was an active user—my college-aged baby brother. My brother was never one to talk on the phone with me and he wasn't into texting me either. Sometimes it took him days to reply to one of my Big Sister check-in messages. But when I sent my first Snap to him, I saw him replying almost immediately. Whoa, this was big! What kind of witchcraft did this magical app possess that would make my brother communicate with such immediacy? That's when I knew there was something really different about this platform. Since the majority of my friends didn't use Snapchat, adding my existing phone's contacts wasn't going to take me too far. I searched the interwebs for blogs and conferences that featured Snapchatters as experts, influencers, or people to follow, and added them. I found third party Snapchat user directories (GhostCodes.com and Snapdex.com) that categorized users by interest or profession, and downloaded more codes.

Eventually, most of the accounts I added were suggested to me by other Snapchannels I followed. Because the Snapchat community understood that discoverability was a major challenge within the platform, they would often share other users' codes and usernames (a practice called "shout outs"). This method was the most reliable way for me to connect with other users, who might share interests with me, and were already vetted by other users. If I didn't know someone but they were recommended by a friend, then they were probably legit—it was the app's own version of curation. It was grassroots organic networking, which meant you couldn't cheat your way through it or pay for views. Just like real life relationships, we had to meet someone through a friend of a friend, and network to find other people interested in the same topics. It was a blank slate, a level playing field where anyone, regardless of celebrity or background, could create a community and a name for themselves.

Over the course of a few months, I had curated my own smallish community of Snapchatters, whose stories I watched, religiously. I enjoyed watching their different lifestyles, and the normal goings-on that occurred in their homes and offices. It wasn't boring or creepy at all, and almost everyone I connected with was over 30 (the typical age range of my personal Snapchat community is 30-55) and DIDN'T send me X-rated pics, contrary to popular belief.

In the early days, I was strictly participating as a voyeur, passively watching other people's Stories rather than engaging with them, but after some weeks, I finally sent someone a comment (a "chat"), and actually got a message in return. I wanted to get to know them, even though, honestly, I felt a little weird sending a message to someone who didn't know me. It took me a while to understand that this was like TV but better—I could actually talk to all of the stars of the show. Wow, so this was a thing—it was like AOL chat rooms, but so much better! It became so normal for me to chat with people through the app that eventually it seemed weird when people *didn't* chat back. The majority of the apps' users utilize the chat functions on a regular basis. Some users choose not to create and public content and only use Snapchat as a messaging tool.

Some friendships grew slowly over time, while others were almost immediate. Some people annoyed me in the beginning, and then their quirks grew on me. Watching their daily stories and listening to their voices provided me with an unexpected sense of comfort. I felt like they were...well...my friends. At first, these people all over the world were just entertainment for me, but then I started to feel like I knew them. Sharing bits and pieces of our history, our passions, our hobbies, and more, fostered a natural progression of developing a friendship that mimicked real life because it was, in fact, real life.

And this is where my story gets really interesting...

■　■　■

## THE MEET UP
Wheels Up!

My one hour and fifteen minute Southwest flight to Salt Lake City, Utah was underway. As a responsible parent and proud hypochondriac, I never imagined that I would be boarding a plane and traveling to another state to spend time with three men and one woman whom I'd never met in person. Heck, I'd never even talked to them on the phone—the only communication we had was through Snapchat.

My mother would not have been pleased.

I "met" Dustin, Shannon, Jason, and Bucky on Snapchat in mid-2016. At this point, we can't exactly remember how all of us found each other, but when we did, we connected immediately because we worked in the same industry. We watched each other's lives every day, learned about each other's kids, pets, and spouses, and before we knew it, we weren't just talking every day, we were talking every day, all day long. We celebrated new babies, new career opportunities, and encouraged each other during challenging times. We shared our expertise and best practices, and helped each other with projects, offering insights without any obligation. The five of us started talking to each other every day, and when I say "talking," I mean Snapping—now, those two things have become one in the same.

We felt like we were actual friends engaging in comfortable conversation, picking up where we left off the day before when we opened our apps. Eventually, we were talking so much and so often that our spouses wondered whose voices were streaming from our screens. They half-jokingly asked us why we had created a "second family," and wondered why we were so interested in watching the daily lives of perfect strangers. The weird part wasn't that we were talking to people we had never met before; the weird part was that we didn't feel like they were strangers. The camera was the medium that brought us together. We weren't just passively viewing each other's personal broadcast networks, we were participating in them.

We were using the camera to communicate.

After about three months of snapping back and forth, we discussed the possibility of an in-person meet up. Our idea was to come together in the same room to mastermind with each other, share best practices, and have some fun while doing it. The more we talked about it, the more it made sense for us to create a mini-conference where each of us could present on a topic while we live streamed the content to a virtual audience. We marketed the event through Snapchat, set up custom Geofilters and secured a group takeover of a large national Snapchat account in our niche. Five people had come together to do something they had never done before, all because of one little app.

Dustin offered to host the group in Park City, which was one of my favorite towns, so I couldn't resist the invitation. We settled on a date that worked for everyone and bought our airline tickets. Shannon and I opted for separate lodging from the rental cabin where the guys bunked (I planned to bring my husband because, admittedly, I was chicken) and we had an escape plan, just in case. After all, these were people we met online and, worse, from Snapchat.

Once we all landed, our plan was to meet at the Starbucks close to the airport. When we finally all met in person, it was like we had just seen each other a few minutes earlier, and picked up conversations right where we left off. It didn't feel awkward at all—it felt totally comfortable. I remember thinking how bizarre and surreal it was to meet a group of people through Snapchat and then end up traveling together, but I guess that's how you made friends in 2016.

The rest, as they say, is history. It was pretty incredible to connect with people from across the country that I had met on my iPhone. Since then, we've worked together on business projects, traveled to conferences across the country, spoken on stages as a group, cried together, vented to each other, and most importantly shared a ton of laughs. I can truthfully say that they have become some of the closest friends I've ever had—really, they're more like family. Without even knowing it, we had built screen-to-screen relationships one Snap at a time, and we were, in fact, talking in pictures.

It was bizarre to think that talking to people through your mobile device would ever be considered normal, or an accepted method of developing deep relationships. Inspired by this profound experience, I started thinking about how Snapchat was changing how we connected with people so authentically.

These were the questions on my mind:

- How did I come to create such a tight bond with people that I only interacted with on Snapchat?
- What was it about this app that made us feel connected to strangers on the other side of a screen?
- Why did it inspire other platforms to make monumental shifts in their feature products?
- If this worked so well with these friends, could I use Snapchat to create an entire worldwide network of like-minded individuals?

I'm about to make a very bold statement: Snapchat isn't a social media platform, it's a powerful conversation pipeline that allows us to communicate with one person or hundreds in real time, amplify our brands, and create engaged communities.

Remember, you don't have to believe something for it to be true.

> *"The real power of Snapchat is in the relationship building. When I created a Snapchat account, I fully expected to advertise and market to the end consumer, like most other social platforms. But what I quickly found is that Snapchat is a POWERFUL way to build genuine relationships and friendships with people, including your potential clients. It's better than I ever thought possible."*
>
> @DUSTINBROHM, DUSTIN BROHM: REALTOR, BLOGGER, SPEAKER

> *"Snapchat's power is forcing most users to be their authentic self to grow a following. In a time when most Social Media channels foster "personalities," snapchat is rooted in reality. This helps people make meaningful connections with each other, along with brands and their customers. To this day it is the only social channel that has created real world friendships for me."*
>
> @REALESTATECIO, JASON FRAZIER: REAL ESTATE MARKETER, CX ADVISOR

> *"The connections I have made on social media, and in particular Snapchat, have been astonishing and life changing. It is amazing to witness how total strangers have become my biggest supporters and have transformed into lifelong friendships. I have been given opportunities to travel to meet many of these new friends, which has also provided me with a new sense of adventure!"*
>
> @RVAHOMETEAM, SHANNON MILLIGAN: REALTOR, BLOGGER, SPEAKER

*"I get to understand people's lives by getting to watch them as they document their lives daily. It makes friendships even cooler because I never thought that I would be making them via a video on my phone. It's broken down the walls of my town so that I can reach anyone in the world."*

@BUCKYBEEMAN, BUCKY BEEMAN: COMMERCIAL
BROKER, VLOGGER, SPEAKER

# PART 1
## THE DISRUPTIVE FORCES OF SNAPCHAT

# 1

## "Alexa, What Is Disruption?"

*"People are very open minded about new things, as long as they're exactly like the old ones."*

— CHARLES KETTERING, AMERICAN INVENTOR

Once upon a time, people worked in offices and developed products to sell in brick and mortar stores. They didn't have to create value, they just had to make their commodity functional. Competition was minimal, and advertisers controlled the sales and marketing process from start to finish. Consumers were at the mercy of sales people who decided what information they wanted you to know. Unless it was in a catalog, a storefront, or your neighbor's home, you didn't know about it.

Of course, we know how this story ends. The internet was invented, and changed how we do just about everything—from how we communicate, to how we purchase, and how we learn. In its short lifespan, the internet has revolutionized centuries old industries and institutions, worldwide. Nearly every Fortune 500 company that originated in 1955 no longer exists; they've either been acquired, merged, or blindsided with bankruptcy because shareholder pressures were making boardroom decisions. They clung to "proven" formulas and stale marketing strategies, choosing short term solutions for long term problems. You could argue that it was bureaucracy or ego that collapsed these companies, or we could just agree that change happens, often inconveniently.

Almost every day, we hear about the Uberfication of "X" industry and read articles about artificial intelligence taking over our jobs. Headlines about the demise of too-big-to-fail companies like Blockbuster and Borders remind us that old ideas about consumption have been thrown out the window. Authors, Ahmed and Olander, eloquently and humorously stated in their book, *Velocity: The Seven New Laws for a World Gone Digital*[3], that, "a Smith and Wesson always beats four aces." Even if you are convinced the deck is stacked in your favor, no company is too big to be out-innovated.

There's nothing funny about an industry collapse, and it doesn't help that the lessons learned are forgotten all too soon. What businesses failed to realize was that technology wasn't the major change—it was our expectations. In the end, the biggest threat these companies ever faced was complacency, and they didn't even know it.

We now live in an era where Amazon Prime has not only become a verb but also a strong behavioral trigger. We want to "Prime" everything in our lives—if I can't buy something with Prime shipping, anymore, I won't even make a purchase. On demand apps are the modern-day Pavlovian conditioning—we use an app, it makes life easier for us (even if we pay more for the service), and the more we use the service, the more we come to rely upon it.

We're routinely self-educating and self-diagnosing online while signing in to new communities, building digital profiles (intentionally or by default), and adding new followers almost compulsively. We're cord-cutting and raising digital natives that intuitively navigate smart devices. Alexa lives on our kitchen countertops, her software learning to respond to our voice commands. We've come to accept the ubiquity of the Internet of Things and define today's terms of service by immediacy and mobile access. We've got apps and access, so we're in control. Powered by Google, anything we want to know, do, or buy can be found within a few keystrokes or thumb swipes. We've entered into a new kind of industrial revolution, in which advances in tech occur at exponential rates.

The dictionary defines "disruption" as a forcible separation or division—two words that often carry a negative connotation. However, disruption can be a powerfully positive force that creates new opportunities and brings communities together. Innovative or disruptive (whatever you want to call it) Snapchat was a catalyst for change in every social media platform. The app's disruptive features opened up Pandora's Box, which caused users to ask more from it than they had in other social networks. It's kind of like flying first class—once you've experienced that extra legroom and free snacks, it's awfully hard to go back to coach.

In the end, disruption is just a ten letter word for change.

## RIDICULOUS OR REMARKABLE?

New ideas sometimes sound plain ridiculous at first. When three college kids developed an app for disappearing photos, no one really thought too much about it. Not even the founders could have predicted the end result of over 170 million daily users, and an eight-digit IPO valuation. Debuting in 2011, Snapchat was a hit with MillenGen who wanted to escape the very public platforms they shared with their parents. What started out as a ridiculous iPhone app that, "lets you and your boyfriend send photos for peeks and not keeps[4]," evolved into a legitimate social network.

Explaining Snapchat to someone who's never used it before is difficult. It's almost as challenging as explaining the legitimacy of renting a room in a stranger's house or giving your address to a total stranger who will pick you up in their personal vehicle. New things always seem a little awkward, until a lot of other people start adopting them, too.

Marketing yogi and prolific bestselling author, Seth Godin, believes that ridiculous ideas[5] are the cornerstone of innovation. In order to be successful, brands must make something remarkable that consumers talk about and share. Godin stressed that appealing to the largest group of consumers possible wasn't going to cut it anymore. Instead, he believes we should focus on attracting fanatical users and taking risks on ideas that speak to a niche audience. He extoled the benefits of risk taking and focusing on early adopters who will spread the word.

In his blog, *SethGodin.com*, Seth writes:

> "If it's *not* ridiculous, it's hard to imagine it resonating with the people who will invest time and energy to spread the word. The magic irony is that the ridiculous plan is actually the most sensible...
>
> We can view the term *ridiculous* as an insult from the keeper of normal, a put-down from the person who seeks to maintain the status quo and avoid even the contemplation of failure.
>
> Or we embrace ridiculous as the sign that maybe, just maybe, we're being generous, daring, creative and silly. You know, remarkable."

Believe it or not, many mainstream products started out targeting one specific segment of the population. Do you think Starbucks had any idea they would someday be selling a multicolored, flavor-changing concoction called the Unicorn Frappuccino when they first opened their doors in 1971? Facebook was originally a website exclusively for university students, and has since become one of the biggest online advertising platforms in the universe.

Let me remind you that odd or even laughable ideas have launched multi-billion dollar companies[6]:

- Sleeping on the couch of a stranger's home (Airbnb, now worth $31 billion)
- Texting a stranger to drive to your private residence and pick you up in their own car (Uber, now worth $69 billion)
- Selling books online to people who weren't comfortable using a credit card online (Amazon, now worth $500 billion)
- Subscribe to a DVD rental service that delivers directly to your door (Netflix, now worth $70 billion)
- The most expensive phone ever sold (iPhone sells 554 units/min and makes over $8 billion in PROFITS a quarter)

A selfie-destructing app that changed your voice and overlays bunny masks on your face seemed like an outlandish concept that wasn't suited for longevity or mass audience appeal. So, was Snapchat like these examples—a ridiculous idea that would become remarkable? Was it dumb enough to succeed? I would argue, yes.

Snapchat didn't want to compete with other social players; they wanted to create their own category of social play. Spiegel wasn't competing with other social media apps, he was competing with television.

Snapchat was entertainment.

In my opinion, if it weren't for Snapchat, the changes that we've seen occur in the feature offerings of Facebook and Instagram would not have happened (or at least would have taken a lot longer to develop). Facebook and Instagram felt that communicating in real time with a camera was so important that they made it their mission to change their own platforms to this same model. When one of the most valuable companies in the world sits up and takes notice, that's a pretty good sign that we should pay attention, too.

■　■　■

## MANIACAL GENIUS

Disruption is a major theme in almost every tech-based tale. Snapchat was a trendsetter that began as a seemingly half-baked idea that big brands didn't take seriously. Discussing the disruptive forces of Snapchat is important in establishing how and why the app inspired its biggest competitors to dramatically alter their own features. Snapchat's disruption sparked a high velocity avalanche of innovation, which produced features that will be commonplace, tomorrow.

Typically, innovative movements are steered by charismatic and ambitious individuals who lead with their gut more than their head. Snapchat co-founder and CEO, Evan Spiegel, believed in disrupting the way we communicate. Spiegel wanted Snapchat to change the way people interacted in real time, both publically and privately. He didn't want to compete with Facebook and Instagram, he wanted to be in an entirely different category—a camera first, and a social network second. He had all the hallmarks of a quintessential disruptor—secretive, brilliant and a maniacally visionary, like Steve Jobs, Mark Zuckerberg or Elon Musk. He had a vision of users sharing their in-the-moment, unfiltered lives through images and videos. His dedication to creating a product that was more focused on user experience than revenues was both refreshing and unsettling to his competitors.

We used to depend on well-educated sales people to help us make purchasing decisions. Now, we depend on predictive analytics and algorithmic equations. The very goal of advertising and marketing is to anticipate a need or trend before it happens, and position a product or service as the solution to said problem. When we think of the most disruptive products, we look back at our lives before we had them and wonder how we survived.

Consumers don't know what they want until you show it to them. As Henry Ford said, "If I had asked people what they wanted, they would have said faster horses." Millions of Snapchat users had no idea that they had been longing for something different because they didn't know it *could* be any different. Delivering a product that fulfills a need they didn't even know they had is THE ultimate loyalty program.

## The Disruptive Vision

At the age of 24, Evan Spiegel laid out his three-fold business model[7] for Snapchat at the 2015 CODE Conference. The normally elusive CEO described his vision with surprising simplicity. Instead of using industry jargon, the Product Visionary reduced his executive summary to three simple concepts: The camera, content, and communication.

**Camera:** The camera was about capturing our lives in a visual way. Images played a central role in storytelling and Snapchat would become a platform for free and easy personal media creation. For millions of years, humans had been talking in pictures. Snapchat didn't innovate that idea, it just gave humans an easier way to do it. He was deliberate and methodical about this capture product—Spiegel said that he wasn't interested in being the first, but he wanted to be the first to get it right.

> *Camera first communication creates relevance and accelerates trust.*

**Content:** Over half of the apps' users are creating native content every day, proving that Snapchat is more about content creation than curation. Snapchat is a platform founded on user-generated content that gave users a tool to create as much as they wanted, whenever they wanted. Talking to your phone a few years ago would have been frowned upon, but today it's accepted, and tomorrow, it's required.

> *We're communicating through our content—we are the storytellers sharing our lives in real time through images.*

**Communication:** We're living in a time of dynamic social change, where we use technology to scale our communications from one-to-one to one-to-many. It's hard to say whether we are talking more or less, nowadays, but we certainly are talking differently. We can communicate with people around the globe at any time with a broadcast network in the palm of our hands.

> *Snapchat ushered in an era of what I call "arm's-length communication," which means we are closer to people that we ever have been before.*

*Note: Even the layout of the three main screens of the app support this vision. The home screen is the camera, the messaging screen is about communication, and the Stories screen is about content.

## Insecurity Breeds Contempt

As platforms and their functionalities continue to evolve, leading companies exist in a constant state of one-upmanship. Rapidly changing technology coupled with shiny object syndrome keeps consumer attention fleeting, and competition between channels cutthroat. In the last 18 months, I've seen more updates, feature rollouts, and rebranding in social than ever before. It's a visionary showdown to see who can acquire and retain the most daily users, capture the most attention, and deliver the highest stock returns.

Pre-Snapchat, social platforms were primarily a documentation of the past hosted and shared on a public forum. It was more of a broadcast system, rather than a portal for intimate conversation. The standard format was a static feed that could be passively scrolled through. It wasn't dynamic or real time, it was curated noise with hashtags. Don't get me wrong, a lot of us loved social media then, we just didn't know what it *could* be like. Once Snapchat came onto the scene, social existed in the present as well as the past and could be as private as you want.

The phone became a camera, and sharing photos and videos became the new texting.

People were getting "real" on Snapchat, and Facebook took notice—the app had proof of concept, and that was extremely seductive. Facebook noticed that "original sharing" had been on the decline[8] for a while (meaning that Facebookers weren't sharing as much personal content anymore). For that, users had moved on to smaller, more intimate platforms like Snapchat. Consumers had spoken, and they told social media that they wanted to go real and go live. The race was on between the social networks, because if you weren't going live, you were getting left behind. Facebook's solution: buy Snapchat.

They say that imitation is the sincerest form of flattery, or, insecurity. In 2013, Facebook's CEO, Mark Zuckerberg made Snapchat an offer that they *could* (and did) refuse. After Snapchat turned down Facebook's $3 billion[9] bid, Zucks may have felt that if he couldn't join them, he would beat them (I imagined after Snapchat declined his offer, the Harvard dropout clenched his fists with Veruca-Salt-like flair, stomped his feet, and snarled "But I want a Snapchat NOW!!").

Kevin Systrom, CEO of Instagram, publically and unabashedly shared their outright cloning of Snapchat in their own Stories product[10].

> *"I think it would frankly be silly of us is we were to say, "Oh, see that good idea over there that's actually fulfilling a need people have to share more moments of their life? Because one person did that we can't go near that idea."*

> He went on further to say that, *"if we're being honest with ourselves, this is the way the tech industry works, and frankly it's how every industry works. Good ideas start in one place, and they spread across the entire industry. Kudos to Snapchat for being the first to Stories, but it's a format and it's going to be adopted widely across a lot of different platforms."*

No shame in that game, eh?

In 2016, there were enough updates to Facebook, Instagram, and Snapchat to make your head spin. It seemed like every week, a new blog post was published outlining the "5 Changes You Need to Know About [fill in the blank]." Snapchat had something that other platforms wanted—engagement and eyeballs. Snapchat made very big companies feel pretty insecure.

I don't blame the other companies for using Snapchat's disruptive features as inspiration for their own product development. They are, after all, for-profit companies with shareholders clamoring for increasingly higher returns on their investments. Going where the attention is keeps them relevant—the more users they add, the more content is created, and the more content that's created, the more advertising opportunities arise.

Competition was fierce and everyone was making Stories—just remember who made them first.

■　　■　　■

## ADAPT OR DIE
Why spend time talking about adaptability in a book about Snapchat?

Because innovation and adaptability go hand in hand. Without embracing change, we cannot fully experience the innovation.

Ironically, the app built on ephemerality proved that permanence was highly overrated. Regardless of what you call it, disruption, innovation, or evolution, everything eventually changes. Learning to pivot in the quick change world of tech is simply par for the course. The most important part of change isn't necessarily the resulting products and services, but rather the learning opportunities presented during the process that teach us to remain flexible and adaptive. I mentioned that this book was, "the true story of an app that may not exist in a year," because virtually every industry and platform will undergo massive changes at some point. This app wasn't the first to create habits or out-innovate someone else, and it won't be the last. On the contrary, the most important lesson you should take away from this book is that change happens. Evolution is inevitable, and everything is eventually discarded in favor of something newer and better.

The following chapters review Snapchat's disruptive forces and how they changed how we use social media:

1. **Camera first focus**: Images used to communicate
2. **Real time communication**: Shareable, in-the-moment experiences
3. **Disappearing content**: Privacy and attention
4. **Vertical video**: Full-screen and immersive video
5. **Augmented Reality**: Delight, surprise and creative advertising

Let's explore each one in detail.

# 2

## Camera First Communication

*"When you see your children taking a zillion photographs of things that you would never take a picture of, it's because they're using photographs to talk."*

*- EVAN SPIEGEL, CEO SNAP INC.*

### PHOTOGRAPHIC MEMORIES
Photos were different when I was a kid.

When I was six years old, I remember my parents lugging around an enormous neck-strapped camera on every family vacation. We didn't have digital screens; instead, we had tiny, square viewfinders and film that needed to be refrigerated and couldn't go through the airport baggage scanners. Back then, we had no idea what the photos we were snapping would look like until they were printed. We didn't get to filter or delete the images if we didn't like them, and we didn't spend a lot of time crafting the ultimate pose. We just stood there, smiled, and if we got one good shot out of the 36 options, we were satisfied.

We dropped off the film rolls at the one hour photo shop to have them developed and printed. I remember the anticipation I would feel opening the sealed envelope and sorting through its contents. We would thumb through the 4 x 6 glossies until we found one worthy of the mantle, bedside table, or gallery wall. The pictures we took weren't altered in any way, and yet we still framed those memories proudly, and lovingly placed them in keepsake books. We treated them with respect and made pacts with our loved ones that if the house caught fire, we would rescue the photo albums.

When I turned thirteen, my parents gifted me a Polaroid "instant camera" for my birthday, and that was my first experience with immediate gratification—well, semi-immediate. I pointed, clicked, and grabbed at the self-developing film that ejected, hoping that frantically waving those white-bordered images in the air would help them develop even faster (if you were an expert, you may have even put it under your armpit). The best part was that I didn't have to wait for days to see the photos. I didn't even have to leave the house—it was convenient and on demand before that was even a thing.

The problem was that this specialty film was pretty expensive, so my parents didn't want me to use it very often. Back then, you were choosey about the photos you took because they had a price tag. Family photos were oftn shot by a professional studio or photographer and was restricted to an annual event due to the expense of it all. Of course you could take your own photos, but you still had to buy a pricey camera and film, and then pay someone else to develop it. Photographs were an investment that people took seriously because the equipment wasn't cheap, and printing required time and effort. If you're my age or older, you remember these limitations all too well.

Nowadays, we don't think about cameras as a luxury item, they've become a given, an expectation, a required feature. Our phones have a professional quality lens and include a free editing studio, replacing the expensive cameras of yesteryear. Because of this, camera store chains have been liquidated, and big box electronic retailers are not far behind. Why would we need a separate camera when we can take pictures anytime, anywhere, and store them by the thousands on mobile camera rolls, or in the Cloud? Even old school photo albums have been pushed out of production by online sites that will automatically compile photo posts from your favorite social networks, design an entire album, print, and ship it right to your door. Instead of worrying about our printed memories being engulfed in flames, now we only have to worry about buying enough gigabytes of storage.

Free, unlimited photo capabilities means that we accumulate a surplus of personal media in the form of images. Today, we have eight times as many picture takers worldwide than there were 10 years ago[12].

> *"It's predicted there will be 7.5 billion people in the world in 2017, and about 5 billion of them will have a mobile phone. Let's say roughly 80% of those phones have a built-in camera: around 4 billion people. And let's say they take 10 photos per day — that's 3,650 photos per year, per person. That adds up to more than 14 trillion photos annually (14,600,000,000,000).[13]"*
>
> MYLIO.COM

Over 60% of Snapchat users are creating content every day[14]. With nearly 3 billion Snaps created per day, it would take you over 800 years to watch every Snap created in ONLY one 24 hour period. Snapchat also gets more video views than Facebook[15] and YouTube[16] combined (18 billion by May 2017), which is a really big deal that made important people take notice.

Photos themselves are meaningful pieces of personal media, but the act of sharing them with others is what connects us as community members and becomes our language. According to Mary Meeker's 2016 Internet Trends Report[17], Snapchat was a photo sharing machine:

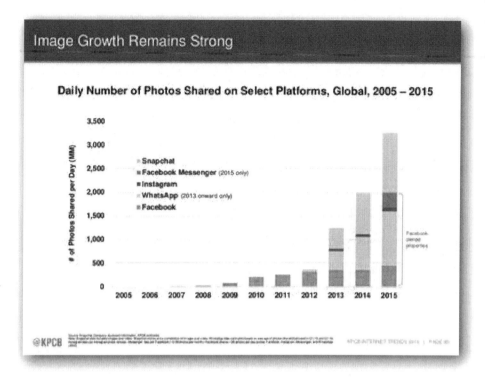

Snapchat's blog[11] sums up how our relationship with images has changed:

"A common thing we hear about social media today is that near-constant picture taking means not 'living in the moment.' *We should put the phone down and just experience life rather than worry ourselves with its documentation.* This sentiment wrongly assumes that documentation and experience are essentially at odds, a conceptual remnant of how we used to think of photography, as an art object, as *content*, rather than what it is often today, less an object and more a sharing of experience. But not all social media are built the same, and I think we can use a distinction in social platforms: those that are based in social *media* versus those that are more fundamentally about *communication*.

The way to understand photography as it happens on social platforms is *not* to compare it to traditional photography, which is about creating an art object, but instead as a communicating of experience itself. It's less making media and more sharing eyes; your view, your experience in the now. The atomizing of the ephemeral flow of lived reality into transmittable objects is the ends of the traditional photograph, but merely the means of the social snap. As photos have become almost comically easy to make, their existence alone as objects isn't special or interesting, rather, they exist more fluidly as communication; a visual discourse more linguistic than formally artistic. As such, social photography should be understood not as a remove from the moment or conversation but a deeply social immersion."

Evan Spiegel understood the intimacy of photographs and their ability to serve as a powerful form of communication. He realized pretty quickly after launching Snapchat that users weren't just taking thousands of random photos a day for keepsakes, they were using them to create dialogue. Selfies weren't simply acts of vanity anymore, they were telling our stories and signaling how we feel.

We're taking more pictures, we just aren't printing them.

Even photos have been disrupted.

■   ■   ■

## THE CAMERA IS THE NEW SOCIAL FEED

Snapchat surprised us by turning the camera into the new social feed. By opening the app to the camera and not a newsfeed, Snapchat gave users a silent call to action to take a photo or video, implying that this app was about *our* visual story. There were no profiles to set up, no cover photos to make, no bios to create—only the camera and access to channels of communication. Users had to swipe left or right to access any other features, which meant they had to intentionally avoid the camera.

The idea that a camera should become the heart of social networking prompted Spiegel et al. to launch a complete rebrand of their company in 2016:

> *"Snap Inc. is a camera company. We believe that reinventing the camera represents our greatest opportunity to improve the way people live and communicate. Our products empower people to express themselves, live in the moment, learn about the world, and have fun together[18]."*

> *- SNAPCHAT.COM*

Snapchat became Snap Inc., and this point of differentiation made a statement. This app wasn't a social media platform—it was a visual storyteller, a communication portal, and an experience-sharing machine. Snapchat wanted users to tell their stories by documenting their lives in images. If you're searching your app store, you won't find it under "social networking." Instead, it's listed under the "camera" section. Snap, Inc. was now a camera company that wasn't even making their own cameras; instead, they were leveraging cameras that already existed in our smartphones.

Our brains process visuals faster, retain them longer, and can use them to experience emotions text doesn't convey. With photos and videos, we could express ourselves on a much deeper level. Snapchat created a platform around visuals to improve the *context* of our content. Watching a personal video from a friend was a better user experience than just reading their status update. We had already succumbed to the Cult of Image, Instagramming our way through meals and filtering our selfies. Expressing ourselves through images wasn't a new concept, we had been doing it for decades, but Snapchat helped us use our images to tell the ultimate life story, and do it in real time.

Some say the rebrand was a creative competitive play to distance their company from other social networks, like Facebook, because, unlike them, it wasn't social media, it was a camera. Whatever their play was, I'd say it was damn smart.

■　　■　　■

## AT AN ARM'S LENGTH

Sharing our daily lives through video and photos is about as intimate as you can get without being in the same physical space as another person. Snapchat ushered in an era of, what I call, literal "arm's-length communication," thanks to the proximity of our mobile devices. Think about it. If someone is speaking with you at an arm's-length, you see eye to eye, comfortably. If you come any closer, it invades personal space, and if you move farther, it's not as intimate. Strangers stand farther apart, while friends stand closer together.

Often carrying a negative connotation, arm's-length used to mean holding another person at a distance, often as a form of protection. Now, this same term accurately and positively describes of the intimacy that our screen-to-screen relationships deliver.

Snapchat was one of the first mobile image-based messaging apps that initiated the personal video era. It changed the way we communicate through the camera, and how we develop intimate communities in a digital world. We share our lives in a series of images, talking in pictures.

In the Snap Inc. SEC Filing pre-IPO, representatives stated that they wanted the camera to be the starting point for their product and conversations within it:

> *"In the way that the flashing cursor became the starting point for most products on desktop computers, we believe that the camera screen will be the starting point for most products on smartphones[19]."*

Luckily, our cameras can still make phone calls.

# 3

## Real Time

*"I stopped watching television because it doesn't talk back"*

*- Chelsea*

### REALITY TV

MTV was a television station that created a distinctive youth culture over a span of 36 years. The concept was simple: create a channel that played music videos 24 hours a day with on-air hosts called Video Jockeys or VJs. It combined two things that every teen already loved—music and television. It was difficult for some executives to embrace a pitch about a music channel targeted at a niche audience of mostly unemployed teens, especially in 1981, because only a very young demographic was interested in watching music on TV (sound familiar?).

But with a deep understanding of their target audience, MTV's outspoken programming and innovative advertising campaigns sold more than just music. Masterfully creating a visual radio, MTV cultivated pop culture icons, and "lifestyle brands," which meant dollar signs for the network and their advertisers.

While it wasn't the first station in history to play music on television, it paved the way to a new visual medium for music and reality programming.

In 1992, an experimental proposal hit the executive's boardroom: "what would happen if a group of seven strangers were picked to live together, work together, and have their lives taped to find out what happened when people stopped being polite and started being real[20]?" MTV's hit sensation, *The Real World*, ushered in the next several decades of non-fiction television trends.

The Real World was perhaps our first experience of user generated content where everyday life could become entertainment for others. We got used to seeing everyday people on television in unscripted roles, though the situations were contrived. Before the days of Real Housewives of Wherever, and the Kardashians, reality TV was more of a behind the scenes look into regular peoples' lives. The idea of being filmed suddenly didn't seem so foreign anymore, in fact, people were lining up to volunteer for shows left and right.

Real people had been on TV before in the form of interviews and documentaries, but no real person had been able to create their own "plot," or be the hero or heroine of their own storyline. Reality TV normalized people watching—we weren't creepy voyeurs or Peeping Toms— and entered us into an era of living out our lives in public (or private), on video. This new TV show genre set off a chain reaction that I can't help but think influenced live social streaming, today.

My fascination with watching the often mundane comings and goings of a group of unemployed 20-somethings on *The Real World* was beyond my mother's comprehension. There was something that made me feel a part of their world. I felt like I might know them in real life and that they could be my friends. They seemed relatable, and relatable was incredible for ratings. The more we saw ourselves in the cast, the more we wanted to watch.

Reality TV created a culture that was comfortable in front of the camera. Almost 30 years after MTV's launch, reality shows are still a thing, they've just changed channels. Instead of tuning in to a specific cable network on our television sets, we open an app and view reality at any time.

■　■　■

## VIDEO MASSACRED THE RADIO STAR

My love for reality TV only intensified when YouTube launched. It was an entire network of relatable people just talking to the camera. It was free, mobile, and I could binge watch to my heart's content. I started watching makeup tutorials and, after some time, found other channels that were suggested to me based on my viewing behaviors. One of the beauty vloggers I watched, Judy Travis of *It's Judy Time* launched a second channel called *It's Judy's Life*[21] that was less about makeup and more about documenting her daily life.

Judy and I happened to be pregnant at the same time. Immediately, I felt like we had a bond. We were both experiencing the very weird world of a changing body, and facing the unknown. I watched her daily vlogs to see what products she bought, how she decorated the nursery, and what her labor was like. I cried when I watched her welcome her first daughter into the world, even though I had never met her in real life.

I remember watching every single video and never missing her daily vlog. I always had something to look forward to and rely on—she never let me down. I held my iPhone in my hand, watching while I was up in the middle of the night with my own newborn son. I truly felt that I had developed some sort of friendship-y feeling for Judy. I was comforted by turning on her channel and knowing that she would be there every time. We were going through the same new mommy struggles, and watching her helped me feel like I wasn't alone.

My husband just shook his head when he saw me watch her videos with my son at our 2 am feeding, rocking away in the glider. He couldn't understand why I felt like I actually knew this stranger on the other side of my device. When I told him about her daily parenting adventures, he would tell me, "Babe, these people aren't real—they're just strangers on the screen, and you don't even know them." But I identified with this human talking to me thru my iPhone.

I felt like she was talking only to me.

There was real power in showing your face and sharing your daily life with people through video. Viewers couldn't help but feel like they knew these creators after watching them so consistently. We became invested in their lives. Instead of fans, we were friends—at least in our minds.

YouTube has replaced television, and in many cases, some social media platforms for young teens. YouTube reaches more 18-49 year olds[23] than any other cable network in the U.S. and more than half of all YouTube views come from a mobile device. Thanks to this free platform, landing a role in a sitcom wasn't the only road to stardom—now you and any of your friends could become Internet famous. We love watching real people.

> *"Some of these videos almost come off like FaceTime or Skype sessions with particularly charismatic friends. And that's how I think their fans—the completists who watch every video and watch them to the end—receive these chunks of content. They're consumed as intensely personal one-on-one dispatches that, paradoxically, often have more reach than many shows on national scale networks[22]."*

> *AdAge.com*

Vlogging has become a legitimate and profitable industry, with over a million YouTubers now earning money from their channels. YouTubers wield enormous influence over viewers, which is why you can attend entire conferences like VidCon[24] to level up your video skills, learn how to grow your subscriber list, and monetize your channel. Creating and editing a video used to be hard work that required us to learn new skills and invest in equipment. Imagine if you could just pull out your phone and hit record and then share it with the world, in real time.

What's better than just watching someone's video?

Talking to someone while they're making it.

■   ■   ■

## AND WE'RE LIVE

Kevin Kelley, futurist and author wrote, "real time is human time[25]." The next best thing to being in the room with someone is going live through our technology. Snapchat was the first "live-ish" mobile platform we had that allowed us to share our lives in the moment with friends. We went from a place of "accumulation" to "instant expression," as described by Spiegel. A few years ago, we could only share experiences and events on social media that had already occurred. We posted photos or videos on social feeds so other people could relive the experience with us, to a certain extent, but it was always in the past. Spiegel used the example of taking photos during a party, and then uploading them to social after the party was over. Yes, his friends and family were able to see the photos and comment, but they couldn't experience it with him as it happened. Real time sharing meant that you could connect with people you cared about in a totally different way.

> *"Now the mobile phone has really empowered this idea of instant expression, which is really showing someone where you are and how you're feeling in the moment. This is important as it relates to identity, because really that's one of the things that's at the core of social media. Accumulation was really about this idea that identity is everything I've*

*ever done, so you have all the pictures of everything you've ever done, and that's who you are as a person. But instant expression changed that, because instant expression says my identity is who I am right now. It says I'm the result of everything I've ever done, but I'm not really the accumulation of all that stuff [26]."*

- EVAN SPIEGEL, CEO SNAP INC.

As evidenced by the chart[27] below, you can see how Snapchat inaugurated the real time trend before any other major social platform:

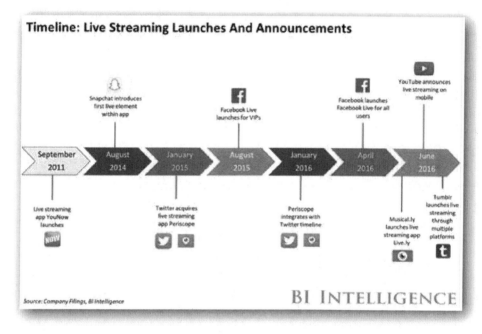

Technically, Snapchat straddles the line when it comes to live video. While it is as current and instant as texting, it's not exactly the same as other live streaming apps like Facebook Live and Instagram Live. In the beginning of Snapchat, users could only share current content. There was no function to access your camera roll (there is now, it's called Memories), so it focused only on real time.

Going live was something everyday people hadn't been able to experience before. Now, we could produce our own "show" and see our audience. We could be in a different country or watch a concert we would never be able to attend. The power of video was amplified because, with a live broadcast, we could participate with the person on the other end of the screen in that exact moment. Live video could be as spontaneous or as planned as we wanted. Not only did it heighten the experience for the viewer, it also intensified a viewer's bond to the broadcaster.

Live video allowed the viewer to become a participant in our stories, and was an incredible equalizer for solopreneurs that felt they couldn't compete with big brands. Anyone could go live without needing a big budget or editing skills. It empowered average individuals by giving them the ability to reach relevant audiences on a monumental scale. Watching videos recorded with a phone also made us much more comfortable with the idea that videos didn't have to be high quality to be enjoyable. Basically, it made us a bit more relaxed about creating content. We could just be spontaneous and share in the moment. Because their default is delete, Stories disappear after 24 hours, which means there isn't a history to review. Stories are what's happening now—current information and experiences.

Today, there is no re-creation needed. No prep work and no extra equipment. During his keynote presentation at the 2014 AXS Partner Summit, Spiegel said:

> *"We no longer have to capture the 'real world' and recreate it online. We simply live and communicate at the same time[28]."*

What we started out calling a live stream really became more like a *life* stream.

# 4

# Disappearing Content

*"Snapchat changed that perception of deleting something as bad. Online typically you delete something if it's bad or if it's really embarrassing. What Snapchat said was if we try to model conversations as they occur they're largely ephemeral. We may try to write down and save the really special moments, but by and large we just try to let everything go."*

*- EVAN SPIEGEL, CEO SNAP INC.*

## PERMANENCE IS OVERRATED

Snapchat's most famous (or infamous) feature was its self-destructing visual, text, and audio messages. Before Snapchat, anything we posted or shared to our social networks was archived, complied, and hoarded. In the early days of Snapchat, there were no double takes, no saving of private messages, and no way to upload content created outside of the app*[1]. Most people couldn't comprehend why anyone would want to create content that didn't stick around, unless it was something you didn't want getting out.

---

1 * Since then, Snapchat made a series of feature changes that allowed users to save and share content if they so choose. Additionally, new smartphone operating systems allow screen recording which means less ephemeral content.

Snapchat's philosophy was that mobile communication should mimic in-person conversations, impermanent unless intentionally recorded. Experiences, conversations, and events are all concepts that exist only in the moment. Talking with friends doesn't exist once the conversation has ended. Just as a Snap disappears, so do our face-to-face interactions.

We are not static beings. We change our styles, our moods, and our minds on a regular basis, which is the essence of why Snapchat didn't believe in trying to save memories. Though we are physically the same person every day, we exist always in a state of change, becoming a slightly different version of ourselves with each passing day. Snapchat's resident sociologist, Nathan Jurgenson, eloquently summarized the concept of what he termed the "liquid self":

> *"The social media profile attempts to convince us that life, in all its ephemeral flow, should also be its simulation; the ephemeral flow of lived experience is to be hacked into a collection of separate, discrete, objects to be shoved into the profile containers. The logic of the profile is that life should be captured, preserved, and put behind glass. It asks us to be collectors of our lives, to create a museum of our self. Moments are chunked off, put in a grid, quantified, and ranked. Permanent social media are based on such profiles, with each being more or less constraining and grid-like. Rethinking permanence means rethinking this kind of social media profile, and it introduces the possibility of a profile not as a collection preserved behind glass but something more living, fluid, and always changing*[29]*."*

Snapchat wasn't anti-permanence, they were simply building a tool that could help us be "in the now" and reflect who we were in the moment. We were using Snapchat to get real, not to go viral.

■　■　■

## ATTENTION AND PRIVACY

Ephemeral content was about two important concepts:

## 1. Attention

Snapchat was just like an original air date for television. We tuned in live because we didn't want to miss our favorite shows, or the resolution to last week's cliffhanger. I remember when I was a tween, I watched Beverly Hills 90210, religiously. The Walshes visited our living rooms every Wednesday night at 8:00 pm Pacific, and I never missed an episode because I knew I wouldn't be able to watch it again unless we "taped" it on the VHS recorder (and who wanted to wait to watch a re-run when you knew all your friends would be talking about what happened at the Peach Pit?!).

Scarcity created urgency and forced users to pay attention. If we know that a product is in limited supply or only available for a specified time period, we are more interested. If someone tells us that we only get one shot to see something before it's gone, we pay attention. That attention was Snapchat's currency, and user engagement was their benchmark for success.

## 2. Privacy

Before the Internet, we had a clear division between who we were at work or in public, and who we were at home. We lived a certain kind of way behind closed doors, and lead with our best foot forward as we entered the public domain. Once you're on social media, the line between public and private becomes blurred, and the idea that nothing is sacred or private can be a bit unnerving to some. We've all read the stories of political figures getting caught with their pants down, haunted by photo leaks and embarrassing tweets they thought they'd deleted. We teach our children that anything they post online will be saved forever, and warn them to carefully curate their timelines before submitting resumes. The permanence of social media postings has entire generations now thinking twice about what they share.

Danah Boyd, Principal Researcher at Microsoft Research and founder of *datasociety.net* studied a social reputation monitoring behavior that involved the self-editing of shared content. Boyd discussed the concept of "whitewalling[30]," which is the act of deleting posts, comments, links, and messages as soon as they've been read in order to keep a public profile's "wall" clean, and prevent archiving. This may seem like going to an extreme measure but allows the user to control their narrative in a most current environment. Snapchat does the whitewalling for you.

Disappearing content meant that we controlled who viewed our Stories. Users took comfort in knowing that they were communicating on their own terms. When you talk with a loved one about an important matter, you don't shout it out in public, you sit down behind closed doors or talk over the phone one-to-one. Privacy is not as closely tied to secrecy as many people think—it's not about what is said, but rather the context in which something is said, where it's said, and to whom. It's about comfort.

Privacy is about feelings.

In a 2014 interview[31] published by *recode.net*, Spiegel told us exactly why Snapchat cares about our feelings:

> *"The one and only way to fight back is with feelings. If we were a data play, we'd have no shot in hell. It's about building something with feelings," Spiegel said. "Desktop computers were about work. This thing in your hand or in your pocket, you want it to feel fun and friendly and comfortable. These are more about feeling. And so we try to establish context, to make people feel comfortable."*

Snapchat ensured users' privacy with the following restrictions:

- No content curation or sharing: No option to download another person's content or share that content outside of the app.

*Note: Originally, you couldn't share someone's Snap with another person in the app, but now Snaps can be "forwarded" to other users. Depending on your privacy settings, others may be able to view those Snaps. There are no notifications sent to the original creator of that shared Snap.

- No forwarding of private chat conversations or images shared in a chat (screenshots can be taken and notification will be sent to participant).

*Note: Text message exchanges (chats) were unable to be saved when Snapchat debuted—they would disappear once the user closed the chat screen. Now, you can press and hold on the message to save it in the chat thread. Videos cannot be saved. Photos and videos can be re-played once.

Ephemeral content turned out to be exactly what consumers didn't know they wanted.

# 5

# Vertical Video

*"A lot of folks in the transition to mobile—which is still ongoing—were taking video that was formatted for livestream desktop and TV, and they were jamming that creative into a mobile feed. That makes sense in the evolution from desktop to mobile, but since we started on mobile, as a blank canvas... our baseline was [we want] full screen. And in order to go full screen, you've got to do vertical."*

*- EVAN SPIEGEL, CEO SNAP INC.*

## EVERYONE GOES VERTICAL

Vertical video is here to stay, and we can thank Snapchat for making it mainstream. There's nothing earth shattering or scientific about why Snapchat went vertical. They did it because they could, and because they did, it set the tone and the orientation for future platforms.

Simply stated, a vertical video is taller than it is wide, or shot in portrait mode instead of landscape. Pre-Snapchat, video experts would have considered shooting vertically to be an amateur move, even taboo. Because we watched video content on a television, computer monitor, or movie screen, horizontal became the universally accepted format.

Snapchat pioneered the vertical video movement for two simple reasons:

1. To make mobile video more engaging and immersive by filling up the entire screen.
2. To accommodate the masses holding their phones vertically 94 percent of the time[32].

As a mobile society, we're spending over 5 hours[33] day on our devices consuming content, almost exclusively holding our phones as they were intended—vertically. According to Mary Meeker's 2015 Internet Trends Report[34], vertical viewing accounted for 29 percent of total view time, a notable increase from the only 5 percent in 2010 (imagine what the vertical viewing time is now).

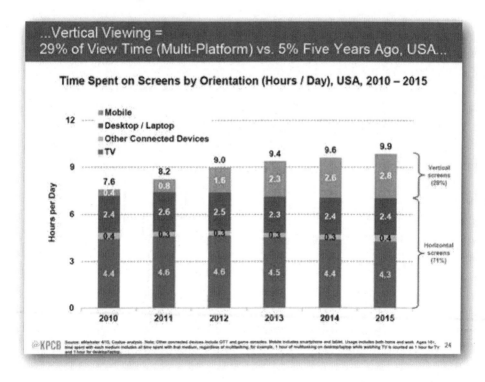

Viewing an image in a full screen format meant that the viewer was totally focused on the content—no comments or distractions above or below, and no barriers to engagement. Vertical was a better user experience and aligned with Snapchat's camera first format. Spiegel wasn't interested in only developing a platform that encouraged users to easily create shareable content, he wanted to provide the very best way for users to consume that content. Vertical video told the best stories and maximized the viewability of the content, while allowing us to fully immerse ourselves without having to make adjustments.

Turned out, Snapchat was onto something.

Once Snapchat came on the scene as THE new format for consumption, it was only a matter of time before this trend became the norm. The tribe had spoken. They said, "we want vertical," and vertical they got. Almost every major platform now supports this format. Some use it exclusively for their latest product features. Making things more efficient, accessible or cheaper increases the likelihood that consumers will continue to use a product. For-profit companies have to listen to what their users want, even if it goes against everything they had done in the past.

### YouTube:
In 2015[35], YouTube updated their mobile platform to support vertical video playback which removed the annoying black "letterboxing" that had previously existed. With more people shooting video on their phones, the platform experienced an increase of vertical uploads. Incidentally, performing a search within YouTube for the keywords "vertical video" yields 6.9 million results.

### Instagram:
Instagram analyzed user photo uploads and found that that 1 in 5 photo[36] and video posts were not in a natively square format. Users wanted

more cinematic and immersive visual experiences, which prompted Instagram to add support for both portrait and landscape content in mid-2015. In November of 2016, Instagram announced that vertical ad formats would also become available. Their Snapchat copycat feature, Instagram Stories, also debuted in the same year and ironically appears only in full screen, vertical format. Currently, Instagram Stories has 200 million users and receives over 150 million views per day.

Vertical seems to be working out well for them.

### Facebook:
In the second half of 2016, Facebook announced, "people enjoy more immersive experiences on Facebook, so we're starting to display a larger portion of each vertical video in News Feed on mobile[37]."

((Eye roll so hard)) Yeah, so we heard.

Basically, when using a vertical format, the image would take up more of the screen area and look bigger than other posts in the Feed. Facebook also reported that vertical video ads were outperforming horizontal and square video ads across multiple countries using the same creative elements, copy, length, audience, and budget. The vertical ads worked better—a lot better. Seventy percent of the vertical video ads, "drove an incremental increase in brand lift, including a three- to nine-point increase in ad recall."

The company's most recent real time video features, Facebook Live and Facebook Stories, only appear in a full screen vertical format.

### Twitter/Periscope:
Periscope, a live streaming app acquired by Twitter in 2015, was gaining some traction and reinforced the fact that people loved vertical video. If you were Scoping on the go, you were almost always vertical—it was just easier to hold our phone or plop it on a tripod. Twitter

also recently announced[38] that 10-second vertical video ads will be rolling out in their curated collection, called Twitter Moments.

■    ■    ■

## VERTICAL AD PERFORMANCE

Snapchat reported that brands using the vertical ad format received 9x higher engagement[39] and completion rates than they did using traditional horizontal formats. Full screen eliminated all other distractions, looked similar to the content that our friends made, and automatically increased a brand's cool factor. Most users felt that vertical ads were less intrusive and viewed brands more positively, generally considering these companies more innovative. It was hard to tell, sometimes, whether a video was an ad or a friend's Snap. Even in Snapchat's professional publishing section called "Discover," partners like Refinery 29 and The Wall Street Journal were allowed to use either horizontal or vertical video content—the performance results clearly proved that vertical was the new black.

> *"Snapchat says its ads garnered twice the visual attention of Facebook, 1.5 times more than Instagram and 1.3 times better than YouTube. When compared to those platforms and TV, Snapchat claims that its ads generated greater emotional response and twice as much purchase intent[40]."*
>
> *— ADWEEK.COM*

No one can debate that Snapchat's advertising team was smart to create ads that looked almost identical to users' content. It's also no coincidence that the same engineers who designed the consumer products also designed the paid products.

Vertical came with some unique challenges, like trying to convince big brands and their heads of marketing to create totally separate content, specifically designed for different dimensions. Brands couldn't easily repurpose video content that had been intended for viewing on a traditional horizontal screen, which meant they had to increase budgets and accommodate logistical differences. It took time for companies to adapt, especially those with an established marketing style. It also meant they would have to get creative and shoot with vertical orientation in mind.

Snapchat advertising teams found that they had to educate[41] top agencies and CMOs at major brands around the globe about the importance of creating visual content with a vertical mindset. Riding the waves of trends, we're seeing new agencies offering niche vertical video consulting services to help brands to navigate the new landscape (pun intended).

> *Note: Just because it may have the right orientation, doesn't mean that every vertical video will be good. The same rules apply regarding making good content.*

Essentially, the reason vertical video has become so popular all boils down to the fact that, more and more, consumers interact with the world through their phones and prefer to save energy by not turning it sideways. Really, what matters most in this case was that Snapchat was the first one to make vertical the norm. Perhaps one of the most compelling reasons that the Snapchat creators decided to only use vertical video was simply because they could.

I suppose it all comes down to perspective, literally.

# 6

## Augmented Reality

*"AR is going to take a while, because there are some really hard technology challenges there. But it will happen, it will happen in a big way, and we will wonder when it does, how we ever lived without it. Like we wonder how we lived without our phone today."*

- TIM COOK, CEO APPLE

### THE FUTURE IS NOW

Snapchat was the first mainstream messaging app to embrace Augmented Reality and figure out a way to make this sophisticated technology fit seamlessly into an everyday user experience. Up to this point, online interaction was about typing on a keyboard or tapping a screen. Now, it could be a surreal multi-dimensional interaction. Once reserved for complex tasks and requiring millions of dollars to access, AR technology was now available to the masses.

Augmented Reality is defined by the Merriam-Webster dictionary[42] as:

"An enhanced version of reality created by the use of technology to overlay digital information on an image of something being viewed through a device (such as a smartphone camera)."

AR is not to be confused with Virtual Reality (VR), which is defined as a totally immersive experience—a completely computer generated interactive environment. Snapchat was the first app that made our selfies more than just a static image—they could be fun, quirky, and creative. Nothing had to be boring anymore—we could animate our environment with 3D digital dinosaurs, digital stickers, and our own hand drawn masterpieces. Giggling at ourselves or watching the faces of children and parents as they experienced a face Lens for the first time was priceless.

Snap's AR features offered users a creative way to inject emotion into their visuals and new ways to provide some additional context to our images. Embellishing a video with your own cartoon likeness (called a Bitmoji) or overlaying text in different colors could make mundane visuals more interesting and shareable. Snapchat made creating content fun and exciting, and gave us a whole new outlook on putting context to our content. We no longer had to rely solely on verbal commentary to communicate where we were or how we were feeling. Storytelling became a much easier and richer process with this AR magic.

AR was also the key to creating the kind of advertising that engaged consumers and *gasp* made them WANT to share it with their network. This kind of advertising was about the user's images and experiences, not just the brand's message. Snapchat realized that if they made people laugh while using a sponsored Lens, it would put them in an open, positive state of mind and they were more likely to connect with that brand and remember it. That's called a massive lift in brand awareness and a major boost to Snapchat's monetization strategy.

Smart.

■　■　■

## FACE LENSES (AKA FILTERS)

If you use Snapchat, chances are you've tried out the face Lenses at least a time or two—come on, you can't help yourself! Changing daily, these digital face-morphing masks tap into our innate curiosity and our love of novelty. It also supplies some major dopamine to the brain when we laugh at our hilarious transformations. Silly or beautifying, the Lenses turn Snapchatters into high-pitched furries or smooths fine lines and wrinkles while enhancing our self-expression. Some users don't Snap at all unless they are using at least one Lens.

(Snapchat Lenses appear at the bottom of the main screen and change daily)

There's a lot of algorithms, patterns, templates, and data processing that take place behind the scenes to make one cute little face Lens. While the result is silly, the computer visioning technology that's baked into the Snapchat app is quite complex. It also had never been used in a mobile app, especially in real time.

The engineering behind Snapchat's filters came from their acquisition of a Ukrainian startup called Looksery[43]. Their patent-pending computer code used pixel data from our phone's camera to "recognize" images, specifically faces, and identify facial data points in order to overlay the effects onto our faces. On a more basic level, this is how Facebook knows which one of your friends is in a picture with you and also why digital cameras place a box around people's faces when you take a photo. The tricky part is taking into account three dimensional space and how an object moves within that space. The software has to be able to recognize the facial movements, such as opening your mouth or raising your eyebrows, because those actions serve as a trigger that activates the animated features of the filters. For example, when using the Snapchat dog face filter, opening your mouth activates the big pink tongue to lick the screen.

Looksery created a Kickstarter campaign in 2013[44] to bankroll their face-altering mobile video technology. Originally, Looksery was hoping to raise $30,000 via its online crowdfunding efforts. Snapchat reportedly purchased the company for over $150 million. I'd say they did quite a bit better than expected. Snapchat also acquired Cimagine[46], an Israeli AR company that developed software that allows you to view virtual objects in any location, in real time. Imagine that you are buying a home and are shopping in a furniture store—you could use this technology to view the couch you are considering in your own living room. Sounds like Snap may be one of the first companies to debut

"Augmented Commerce." Since then, Spiegel & Co. continue to snap up noteworthy AR companies and catapult them into the future.

Earlier this year, Snapchat pushed father into the AR space by launching "World Lenses[45]," which meant that your environment could join in on the AR fun, too. Before they were introduced, Lenses were only available for faces and had to be accessed through the front-facing camera. Now, by using the rear-facing camera, 3D Lenses could alter the world around you in a creative way. Activating a World Lens allowed users to decorate their living room with 3D objects like Bitmojis, rainbows, and cute animals. The digital stickers behaved as they would in the real world. For example, if you walk closer to the AR object, it gets bigger. Pretty trippy. Most people say disappearing content was Snapchat's claim to fame, I say its AR, and they've barely scratched the surface of what's possible.

Lenses became a major source of advertising dollars for the app and an easy way for brands to capture hundreds of millions of eyeballs. Because Lenses were able to alter our appearances or create a new interactive environment, that innovation lead the way for advertising that was more engaging than typical campaigns. In 2015, Snapchat expected that brand sponsored Lenses (advertisements disguised as filters) to reached upwards of 16 million views per DAY[47].

Sponsored face Lenses offered an unobtrusive advertising medium that allowed consumers to engage with a brand on their own terms and in a very fun way. Most of us hate ads and know when we're being sold, but don't mind as much if we're having fun as a direct result of an ad. Because the ad is about taking selfies with a Lens or filter (read: I am at the center), users were willing to play a part in the marketing campaign.

Snapchat describes the power of a sponsored Lens on their website:

*"Lenses are a completely new take on brand activation, and one of our most engaging ad products. Lenses offer not just an impression, but "play time"—the time Snapchatters spend playing with the interactive ad you've created. We believe that when you're feeling playful, you're feeling open-minded, which contributes to Sponsored Lenses' effectiveness[48]. "*

The magic wasn't just in the user experience, it was the compounded effect of users sharing their own content, overlaid with a brand's paid ad. Brands that use augmented reality to advertise stand a much better chance of consumer engagement and boosting awareness thru the power of the share. Snapchat's sponsored Lenses were a brilliant monetization play because millions of users were engaging *voluntarily* with the ads and then sharing those images with their personal networks. Exposure on a massive scale is worth the high price tag, as millions of people sharing their Snaps creates exponential or viral viewership.

The value of the Lens or filter wasn't just in the number of people that interacted with these AR features. It was more about the mass sharing of images that included their branding. Paying a premium to reach that many ENGAGED people is exponentially more valuable to a brand than running a television commercial that most people won't even see because they're either looking at their phones, or fast forwarding to get to their show. Furthermore, brands could experience a compounding effect as people shared their images within their networks.

A sponsored Lens can require up to eight weeks of creative development and cost[49] (on average) between $275,000 and $800,000, depending on the day of the week, and if it's being used for a holiday or special event, like the Super Bowl or the Oscars. According to an Adweek.com article, Taco Bell paid top dollar to create a sponsored Lens that ran during Cinco de Mayo, turning users' faces into a giant taco, and received 224 million impressions. Even more interesting, the average user played with the Lens for 24 seconds before sending it to a friend.

*"In terms of unique plays—or the number of times individual people interacted with the ad—the campaign generated 12.5 years' worth of play in a day, according to Snapchat[50]."*

*— AdWeek.com*

Movie studios have also begun to incorporate these sponsored Lenses into their marketing strategy is an attempt to reach an audience that no longer watch television commercials. *X-Men: Apocalypse* made a bold and brilliant marketing move by taking over ALL of the Snapchat Lenses for 24 hours. (Yep, they even replaced the flower crown and our favorite pooch.)

*"By the end of the takeover, the Lenses received over 251 million plays and 298 million views. Snapchatters spent an average of 109 seconds playing as the movie's characters, resulting in 56 years' worth of play in a single day—a testament to the level of engagement the Lenses inspire[51]."*

*— AdWeek.com*

■　■　■

## GEOFILTERS

Geofilters are location-specific graphics (think: digital sticker) that users can overlay onto a photo or video Snap to add more context and visual interest. For example, if you are vacationing in Hawaii, you might Snap a photo on the beach and add a Geofilter that shows the name of beach you are visiting. As long as you have your phone's location services turned on, Snapchat allows you to access these Geofilters at thousands of places around the world. Snapchat's geo-location data is powered by Foursquare, and uses Wi-Fi, Bluetooth and GPS signals to essentially map the world. Geofilters are not nearly as fun and interactive as a face Lens, but they are still a simplified version of AR, as are the text and drawing features.

Photo Credit: Snapchat.com

These filters can also be "sponsored," meaning that advertisers pay to create special filters that are actually advertisements. Users don't have to interact with the brand directly or take the time to look up information, they only have to select a filter and go. Thanks to the incredibly accurate location data, advertisers are able to get very specific about where their ads were placed—over a sporting event, a music festival, etc. A sponsored Geofilter[52] delivered to a national audience will typically be seen by 40% to 60% of daily Snapchatters, and has been proven to drive a lift in brand recall and awareness, according to Snap, Inc. research.

By creating a Geofilter, big brands and everyday people are able to create brand awareness as users swipe left, select their filter, and share that photo with their network. Snapchat eventually made the smart financial decision to allow the public to create their own custom "On Demand" Geofilters through their website. Now, users can even create their own custom Geofilters right inside of the app itself, and complete the entire design and payment process from their phones. Now anyone with a Snapchat account can create a custom design for any occasion in a few simple clicks with zero graphic design experience required.

■　■　■

## SPECTACLES AND FUTURE AR

Snapchat wanted to take sharing our visual experiences to a whole new level. They envisioned a world where we could share our perspective so that it felt like we were there. This idea was the impetus for the invention of their video recording sunglasses called Spectacles. These mega-hyped sunglasses were stylish enough to wear without getting made fun of, and allowed you to share your personal point of view, hands free, with a cool 115-degree periphery that felt like human vision—talk about immersive.

Not only were these face cameras designed to share a wearer's point of view, they were created to eventually serve up virtual ads and experiences. Future Snap wearable devices may include watches, visors, helmets, and other attachments. Snap has also reportedly hired a staff of well-known AR specialists with impressive visual effects resumes that include blockbuster movies like *Iron Man*, *Pirates of the Caribbean*, and *Superman Returns*[53].

Snapchat will continue to patent specific features of their proprietary tech, and invest in hardware like Spectacles to create more attainable platforms for their AR services. Imagine walking through the mall with your Spectacles on, or opening Snapchat and viewing all of the discounts, coupons, and reviews available for every product. Spiegel believes that they are just at the beginning of what a camera can do, which means we should keep our eyes out for future product launches.

While they haven't divulged much information publically about their future plans, patents[54] filed in May of 2017 revealed that they're doubling down on augmented reality, as well as "emotion recognition," and a possible real time built-in commerce platform.

I know it sounds like something in the distant future, but just remember, the iPhone didn't exist 10 years ago.

# Part 2
# Snapchat's Psychology

# 7

## An Irresitible App

*"Forming habits is imperative for the survival of many products. As infinite distractions compete for our attention, companies are learning to master novel tactics to stay relevant in users' minds. Amassing millions of users is no longer good enough. Companies increasingly find their economic value is a function of the strength of the habits they create. In order to win the loyalty of their users and create a product that's regularly used, companies must learn not only what compels users to click but also what makes them tick."*

*- Nir Eyal, Author*
*"Hooked: How to Build Habit-Forming Products"*

### CREATURES OF HABIT
Irresistible.

That's the word that every company dreams will be used when describing their product or service. When something is deemed irresistible, it means that instead of being a nice-to-have, it becomes a must-have. The most successful products are the ones we feel compelled to use on a regular basis. These kinds of products relieve those annoying anxious sensations we experience when we're not using them, and when we finally do use them, they delight our brains with a jolt of dopamine, confirming we made the right decision to use again.

While cigarette companies built financial empires on getting users hooked with a physically irresistible product, Apple made the iPhone so psychologically irresistible that we can't imagine living without it. This fits into the larger narrative of companies generating repeat business through various means, including: selling inventions that fill a previously untapped need (television), improving an existing innovation (sliced bread), establishing brand association with the product itself (Kleenex), or drawing upon a product's naturally addictive qualities (again, cigarettes). These products have universal appeal and carve out a niche once people start using them. The products that create heavy users are often the ones that survive disruption. Snapchat calculatingly designed their product around the principles of habit formation and social psychology to keep users returning day after day, sometimes hour after hour, to get their fix.

| 158 million daily users | 2.5 billion Snaps a day | over 60% of users Snap daily |

## SNAP STATS

| On average, users visit 18x per day | over 25% of daily users post to their Story | on average, users spend 25-30 minutes |

(Data Source: Snap, Inc. SEC
Filing, February 2017)

Snapchat experienced a meteoric acquisition of daily active users, and according to Apple, was the number one most downloaded app in 2016[55]. Snapchat was generating 10 billion video views a day, double the views of the go-to platform for video, YouTube, and higher than Facebook. Snapchat grew so quickly that in its first four years in existence, it added more new users than any of its competitors over the same time period[56].
It was as if people were becoming *addicted*.

A habit is a behavior that is repeated so often that it becomes automatic or subconscious. On average, we're making over 35,000 decisions a day[57], and we have to create mental shortcuts that will simultaneously help save us time and keep us safe. Our brains conveniently store memories of experiences, and categorize them into specific areas for quick access in the future. When faced with a new experience, our brains search through those memories and refer back to them to decide what to do next. If we survived the day before, then our brains tell us we should perform a similar routine today.

Many of our modern behaviors descend from this biology, even if they have nothing to do with actual survival. Waking up in the morning and reaching for your smartphone to scroll through the Feed is a habit. Checking your Instagram messages or email inbox multiple times a day is a habit. Checking your iPhone for messages, even though you haven't heard it buzz, is a habit.

While not as obvious as some physical responses we normally associate with addictive behaviors (smoking, overeating, etc.), social media apps often leverage powerful psychological responses that habituate our permanent behaviors. Thanks to neurochemical reactions, our brains light up when we open a message, just like when you take a hit of cocaine. We experience a rush of dopamine also known as the "reward molecule[58]" that makes us feel good. It's also why we're junkies for uncertainty, and love the thrill of not knowing what's coming next.

We unconsciously seek out novel experiences that will stimulate those pleasure seeking neurons. Every time we see a message notification, we feel compelled to open it. It's not just the reward of opening the message itself, but the search for the next possible reward that keeps us going. This seeking behavior is exactly why we love Snapchat's face Lenses. By making users giggle in delight, Snapchat knew they would be activating powerful psychological motivators that would keep us coming back for more. Admit it—even if you are a staunch face Lens hater, you still scroll through them just in case—we can't help ourselves. Whether it's boredom, depression, or happiness, we modulate our moods by executing these habits.

Snapchat ticks off all the marks on the habit formation checklist. It serves us continual triggers that create habitual behaviors, seducing us with each and every log in. We never know exactly what we're going to get, so we continue the seeking cycle.

It feels good, so we want more.

■　■　■

## HOOKED

Nir Eyal, author of *Hooked: How to Build Habit-Forming Product*[59], is an expert in "behavioral design," which is described as the intersection of technology, business, and psychology in the process of habit formation. His work helps companies understand how to design products and services that will create beneficial behaviors (habits) in users by delivering a highly engaging user experience, with a sprinkle of neuroscience thrown in for good measure. His work is all about using mind control for good, not evil. With a professional background in the video gaming and advertising industries, Eyal is well-versed in how to make an irresistible product.

Eyal's research on human behavior and psychology led to the creation of his "Hook Model," which is helpful in explaining the Snapchat addiction. The Hook Model explains the cycle of behavioral triggers and responses that, when repeated consistently, will establish a habit. According to Eyal, a Hook is how companies can "manufacture desire" by solving users' problems with their product so frequently that it results in "unprompted user engagement[60]." Basically, that means that when a company uses a Hook Model, they don't need to advertise to keep users coming back.

Let's explore how Snapchat uses the Hook Model:

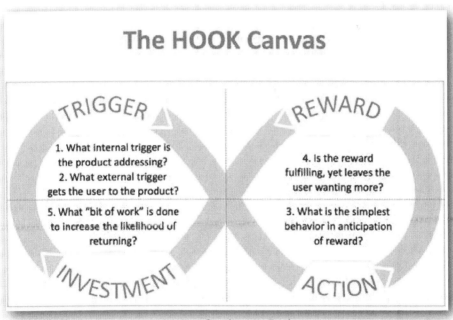

Image Credit: Nir Eyal

## 1. **Trigger**

The first part of the Hook Model is the Trigger. There are two types of triggers, external and internal.

**EXTERNAL** triggers are the notifications on your apps that give you a prompt for what to do next. By opening and reading the message, you then know how to reply, and what tone and words to use. When we see this kind of trigger, we typically feel anxious until we take an action.

Examples of external triggers in Snapchat:

- **Message notifications**: We can't see a preview of the message in Snapchat like we can when someone sends us a text message, and that activates our curiosity. We want to open it to find out what it says. Once we open the message, we process that information and create a response based on the message received. Often, we feel obligated to reply because we know that the sender can tell that we've opened their message.
- **Shout-outs** (when someone shares your Snapcode or username): We feel flattered and grateful, and often feel as though we should return the favor, or at minimum, say, "thank you." This is the basic law of reciprocity.
- **Views**: Similar to the above. When we see that someone has watched our Story, we may feel an obligation to watch theirs.
- **New "add" notification**: Naturally, many people will want to return the favor, so to speak, and "add back" that person's account. The adding process often triggers curiosity which prompts us to watch their Story and learn more about their content. This person could be a potential new friend.
- **Story preview thumbnail**: Viewing the small circle image of someone's Story in the feed peaks our interest—what have they been up to?

*Note: Earlier this year, Snapchat removed the countdown timer, which indicated the remaining length of someone's Story. I assume they did this to increase Story view completion, watch time, and engagement. The timer itself had become a trigger because it caused some people to skip past a user's Story if they saw the timer and felt it was too long.

**INTERNAL** triggers are the feelings we experience that make us want to avoid something or gain something. We respond to these triggers by drawing upon memories of what we have learned from past experience. Feeling like you are missing out on something by not watching your friends' Snapchat Stories creates a sense of discomfort or anxiety, and those internal feelings manifest into an external behavior. These are the kind of triggers that create FOMO (Fear of Missing Out). What's happening with my friends on their vacation? Did I get any new likes on my Instagram posts? Did anyone message me about my funny Snap? We want to relieve our internal anxiety so we repeat behaviors that have quelled these uncomfortable feelings in the past, like checking our notifications. When we receive feedback and positive reinforcement, it reaffirms our actions and helps guide us in the right direction.

Habit-forming products often start off with external triggers that encourage people to use the product. Eventually, with the continued use of the product, internal triggers take over, and that's when a habit is formed. In the beginning, you might check in on a friend's Story from time to time, but when you begin engaging more deeply with a community and creating friendships, you become much more invested and that message notification is no longer the main driver of opening the app—it's how that notification makes you *feel*.

Examples of internal triggers in Snapchat:

- **Boredom**: Checking friends' Stories is entertainment and makes time go by faster.

- **Loneliness**: We can view friends' Stories from all over the world. We're immediately sharing their experiences and can become a part of their Story by commenting on their Snaps. We no longer feel alone when we can watch and talk to our community.
- **Belongingness**: We can watch Stories from people who are like us, going through similar scenarios, and that makes us feel connected to them. We can also participate in Snapchat themed games on specific channels like "Frozen Snap Friday" or "Thankful Thursday," where groups of users can connect using a common theme. We are now participating within a community. Our perceived self-worth is validated as we feel accepted by others.
- **Reciprocity**: We want to support our friends, which triggers us to watch their Stories and participate.
- **Fear of Missing Out (FOMO):** Disappearing content is the perfect scarcity trigger. We're compelled to check in daily so we don't miss any of the storyline. We may also view others in our community talking about something that a mutual Snapchat friend shared on their account, and we don't want to be left out of the loop, so we check in. Simply watching friends having fun using the latest Lens or filters may become a trigger that makes you want to try them out, yourself. Similarly, we use it to avoid fear. We don't want to lose a memorable moment that we want to share with others, so we take a Snap and post it to our Story. Or, we're afraid people may stop watching if we don't post regularly, so we feel compelled to create content consistently.

## FOMO Sells Specs

*In an effort to take sharing our perspective with the world one step further, Snap Inc. created Snapchat-enabled camera glasses, called Spectacles, which not only recorded video, but also looked pretty darn slick. Snap, Inc. positioned these camcorder specs as* an experimental "toy" and not as a piece of high tech equipment, amplifying their fun and games theme.

Snapchat's approach to marketing "Spectacles" was one of the best uses of the FOMO that I've ever experienced. If you were a child or parent in the eighties, you remember limited supplies of Cabbage Patch Dolls and Teddy Ruxpins flying off the Toys R Us shelves. Spectacles is the modern day Cabbage Patch Doll.

The marketing of Spectacles was pure psychological genius. They didn't create a boring website to sell stock; instead, they manufactured friendly-looking dispensing stations called Snapbots that looked like if a Minion ate a vending machine. The Scarcity principle was in full effect as Snapbots61 were secretively dropped in mystery locations across the United States, one of them at the Rose Bowl stadium, and even near the Grand Canyon. Pop up stores attracted throngs of Snappers, and people who had never even used the app, but knew they could resell them on eBay for a profit. Tweets rang out about the latest Snapbot sightings, and you hoped that by the time you got there, the machine wouldn't be sold out. We were awed with their creativity (I, personally paid triple the ticket price to get a pair on eBay).

You couldn't even use the tech side of Spectacles unless you use Snapchat, too—they don't connect with anything else. So, waiting in lines, or spending three times the money to buy them on eBay before they were sold online, meant that you had to be a fan of the app. Obviously, selling a few pairs of Spectacles at a time wasn't going to rake in the dough for Snapchat—it had nothing to do with money and everything to do with creating a buzz. Snap wanted to have fun with their fans. They created a game that sent people "on the hunt." There was a method to their madness, after all.

What made Spectacles so addicting? The hype.

## 2. **Action**
The action is our response to a trigger.

When it comes to creating habits, the more we take an action that is successful, the more likely we are to continue to repeat those actions in the future—it's not just how many times we repeat something that impacts the habit formation. It's also about how easy it is for the user to take an action in response to the trigger, that increases the likelihood that a habit will form. Our brains are looking for shortcuts, so if we don't have to think as much about what we're doing, we're likely to continue that action. Snapchat streamlined the user experience by making it quick and easy to create content and enhance it with filters. There's no swiping through screens to access the camera. Simply open the app and Snap away. Once the Snap is created, a large blue arrow appears which makes sharing that Snap effortless. It's these small but impactful features that facilitate the habit and make Snapping an extension of your normal daily routine.

Examples of actions (in response to triggers) in Snapchat:

- Receive a message: **action** > open it
- Receive a troll message: **action** > block the user
- Watch a friend using a funny Lens: **action** > use it yourself
- Viewing a friend's Story preview thumbnail: **action** > watch their Story
- Someone adds your account: **action** > add back

## 3. **Reward**
Each time we take an action ignited by a trigger, we receive a reward that relieves stress, makes us happy or can even help us avoid a negative experience. Once we receive that reward, it makes us want more. It's why we like posting photos on Facebook and receiving "likes" and comments. The most important part of the reward is that it is variable, meaning it isn't the same exact reward every time. Variability keeps

our brain from knowing what will happen next, which is why we love reading a book or watching a movie for the first time. After we've seen the ending, we are less likely to re-read or re-watch because we know what's going to happen. Novelty and uncertainty are two things that our brains inherently love, which is why Snapchat frequently changes the Lenses, Stickers and Geofilters. This is also why gambling is so addictive. You could win a small amount or a very large amount, but you won't know until you try.

Examples of rewards in Snapchat:

- Receiving positive comments on your Snaps encourages you to create similar content in the future. You may begin to intentionally craft specific content based on what you believe your viewers will enjoy and, in turn, that gives you an internal reward— a sense of pride and proof that you are valuable to the community.
- When we view others' Stories, we receive the reward of being "in the know." The ultimate variable reward is watching a new Story each and every day.
- We send messages to others to encourage replies. Seeing those notifications can make us feel loved or heard.
- Watching every Story in your feed allows you to feel in control and accomplished. It's the same reason we love completing to-do lists and achieving a zero inbox.
- We participate in (or create our own) theme days and games to connect with community members. We feel valued as the connector because we never know who will participate, or whether new people will join.
- When we find an article, video, or Snapchannel that we think is valuable or entertaining, we have an immediate urge to share that with our community. When someone finds value in something we've shared, they relate that value back to us, which

perpetuates a positive feedback loop that makes us want to continue sharing in the future.

*Note: Trolls especially love a good variable reward. With each direct message, they hope that someone will respond. It could be a negative response or a positive one, either way, they got what they came for.

## 4. Investment

The more time and energy we invest into something—a project, a community, or a platform, the more value we place on that thing. After a while, many users of any platform believe that leaving and starting over is too much work, since they've already invested so much of their time growing a community and a brand within one network. That's what every social network is hoping will happen—they want you to become so engrossed in that ecosystem that you never want to leave. At the very least, they want it to be slightly painful to leave, so in the end, you'll just throw your hands up and say, "never mind."

Some refer to this behavioral theory of investment as the "Sunk Cost Fallacy[62]." David McRaney, creator of *YouAreNotSoSmart.com*, articulates this idea as follows:

> *"The Misconception: You make rational decisions based on the future value of objects, investments and experiences.*
>
> *The Truth: Your decisions are tainted by the emotional investments you accumulate, and the more you invest in something the harder it becomes to abandon it."*

Examples of investment in Snapchat:

- The more content you make, the more engagement you get, so you feel the need to be consistent, and keep engaging with others.

*Note: What is most interesting to me is that many regular Snapchatters make public apologies when they have been unable to Snap as much as they have in the past. It's almost as if they feel an obligation to their community, and think they have disappointed them if they don't provide the same level of content that they normally do.

- The more conversations you have with people, the more likely you are to watch their Stories, and the more you watch their Stories, the more invested you become in their lives. This makes you want to continue watching their Stories, and also makes it more likely that you will use the app to talk to them.
- You've spent time organically growing your community, you don't want to start over on another app because it seems overwhelming.
- You've become adept at using Snapchat and all of its features and creative elements, so you want to continue using it now that you have mastery of it. We're less likely to want to learn the ins and outs of an entirely new platform.

In my opinion, Snapchat wants people to work for it—they know that when humans invest time into learning something new, they are more likely to continue to use it in the future. The Holy Grail of social media platforms and apps is the Daily Active User. The more people that use an app and continue to use it on a regular basis, the more opportunities for monetization.

Snapchat, Instagram, and Facebook are today's dealers pushing our tech drugs of choice. We want it all day, every day, and God help us if we don't have Wi-Fi. Snapchat scientifically focused on product psychology and how its features would improve user experience in order to facilitate habitual use. It got people hooked through a series of triggers and rewards, but also by giving them an incredible user experience and delighting them with the unexpected. Because of a maniacal focus on the user experience, fun, creativity, and connection, Snapchat made it nearly impossible to quit it once you got in deep.

Snapchat is a hardcore habit.

# 8

## The Psychology Of Snapchat

### WE'VE GOT NEEDS

In my opinion, other platforms are focused on gaining followers and getting likes, while Snapchat is more focused on getting to know people. The specific real time communication aspect within a private setting accelerates community building.

In their book, *The Social Organism: A Radical Understanding of Social Media to Transform Your Business and Life*[63], authors Luckett and Casey theorize that a digital world of videos, posts, and hashtags function symbiotically, as if they were a living organism. The book goes as far as to compare microbiology, cellular structure, and metabolic qualities of an organism to the ecosystem of social media. Essentially, they outline a powerful metaphor for how technology and platforms act like a living, breathing society that reaches to the ends of the earth. Their work discusses parallels between social media and bio-pathways (like arteries) in the body. It's a network similar to the biology of veins, nerves, and cells—one that requires nourishment and attention. Just like humans, social networks can have viruses or develop cancerous cells that require us to cut them out, or "block" them. The tech body needs to be fed just like our physical ones. It needs content like we need nutrients, and demands stimuli like we require touch and love.

Social media has only been accepted as mainstream for a little less than a decade. What once was an afterthought or something "the kids do" is now a legitimate conduit for connection and business. Technology and social media have created a global neighborhood where it doesn't seem like we're so far apart. Billions of people all over the world share their lives in updates, posts, and messages with one common denominator: community. We want to belong and we want to connect with people.

External triggers become internal after repeated use. Those internal triggers are the ones that really keep us sticky to a product or service. They are the basic drivers of our needs as humans—community and connection. Once habitual behaviors start to form, Snapchat reinforces them by hitting on some deep psychological drivers for us humans. We know it's changed how we communicate cameras and now we'll explore how it's changed the way we develop communities.

## TRIBES

If you sat through any Psychology classes in college, you may remember a theory called Maslow's "hierarchy of needs[64]," which explains what motivates our behaviors. Basic physical requirements like food, water, and shelter are obvious must-haves, but once those needs are met we move on to the secondary needs of feeling safe, a sense of belonging, and of course, our need to feel love. According to Maslow, we humans are a needy bunch. We crave friendship, intimacy, trust, acceptance, and being part of a community to feel whole and reach our fullest potential.

Lack of human connection and empathy has been scientifically proven to lead to depression, which can even manifest into physical ailments. When we don't feel loved, our self-esteem erodes, and we begin to believe we are unworthy of attention. We want to connect with likeminded individuals and become part of a community who understands us—quirks and all. Being a part of a group is about giving as much as receiving. When we contribute to our community, we feel validated and valued. Without belonging to a tribe, we feel lost, misunderstood, and invisible. Without a tribe, our message cannot be heard or make an impact in someone else's life. Alone, we are merely on an island. We can't share our talents nor can we benefit and grow from experiencing others'.

When we hear the word "tribes," many of us think of Seth Godin[65], who literally wrote the book on the subject. However, I love the way author Jeff Goins defines a "tribe" in his blog:

> *"A tribe is a small but powerful group of people. It's a fan base, a Bible study, a group of influencers. A tribe is small enough to feel personal but large enough to make a difference.*
>
> *A tribe is not usually created out of thin air. More often than not, tribes are found. They are existing groups of people formed around very specific interests and passions. Many times, they're leaderless—until someone has the courage to step up."*
>
> *- GoinsWriter.com[66]*

How Snapchat encourages community:

- **It's authentic:** Snapchat mimics real life, because you can't really hack your way through it. You can't buy Likes or hashtag your way to more connections (at least for now), and it's very organic, just like a real life relationship. Watching people that we relate to each and every day in their homes, places of work, and with their families makes an emotional impact. You bond with these people as if you were with them, physically.

  By connecting with people who share our taste, interests, or hobbies, we already feel like we have common ground—a sense of familiarity, even if it's only based on a seemingly inconsequential data point. This relatability factor is what makes us subconsciously like someone wearing the same jersey at the

Super Bowl party. We're part of the same team, even if we don't know each other's names. By design, Disney employees wear nametags that include the name of their hometown, because meeting someone who grew up near you is a pretty powerful psychological connector. Snapchat is the ultimate trust accelerator because it's more difficult to pretend to be someone else on camera for an extended period of time. If you pretend, people see right through it. Snapchat is "in real life."

- **It's intimate**: Small, private groups are how we feel most comfortable in real life. We talk to friends over dinner and share updates about our lives out of the public eye. When we can talk in confidence, we don't have to censor ourselves. But when we're talking on stage to a room full of people, we have to think about what we're saying, just in case we might offend someone. We are afraid to be judged for our opinions and our quirks, but we feel free to be ourselves amongst our small tribe who accepts us as we are.

  Feeling overwhelmed by political rants, global tragedies, cyberbullying, and the pressures of being "edited," a mostly younger audience moved away from the broadcast networks of traditional social media to a more uncensored, raw space. Instead of broadcasting a generic message to a huge amorphous audience, they began "narrowcasting" their lives, essentially communicating with small, intentionally selected groups of people. It's no wonder that younger adopters migrated away from Facebook because their parents couldn't figure out how to use Snapchat. Even if they did, they probably couldn't find your account, and they certainly couldn't see what was being shared. Article link shares, quote memes, and mass appeal news content feels a lot less personal than goofy photos of your friends and family. Over and over, I hear the same thing from people using Snapchat—it just feels more real and more intimate than other platforms.

Snapchat even has a Sociologist on staff, Nathan Jurgenson, who is not only a researcher for Snapchat but also social media theorist. He is best known for his stance against Digital Dualism, or the belief that who we are online and in social media is separate from who we are in "real" life. Both Jurgenson and Spiegel share the belief[67] that the binary concept of a static profile represents a different, unrealistic version of ourselves. This is the idea that we share who we want to be online and hide who we are offline, sharing our true selves with only our most intimate family and friends. It makes sense to me that a company who believes their product is changing behavior would partner with experts in social theory and use that science to shape the future of their software and hardware offerings.

With Snapchat, people felt uninhibited.

- **Messaging behaviors**: According to WeAreSocial.com[68], over half of the world's population now owns a smartphone, and that number continues to grow each year. These devices act as our literal lifelines to the world. I admit, I've frantically searched for my phone in the office or at home shouting out, "have you seen my phone," to anyone within earshot, only to realize that I was holding it in my very own hand. Most of us would rather lose our wallets than our phones, these days. Phantom Vibration Syndrome[69] has become a modern day psychosis, where we are sure we heard our phones vibrate, only to find out that no one has called or messaged. Our ringxiety is not unlike a parent listening for the specific sound of their offspring's yell in a crowd as we wonder, "was that my phone or yours?"

  Messaging is what we do most on our phones, with the average young adult sending over 110 texts per day[70] (and that's not counting within messaging apps. That means people aren't calling or texting others, they are using an app that messages, like Snapchat, Whatsapp, or WeChat. Messaging through an app is a social activity, but it's much more private and done with a specific purpose. We're spending up to 50 percent[71] of our mobile time in apps but not for the same reasons we once did. Today's apps are offering much more than games or updates. We can order transportation, video chat, and even send money.

Today, we are seeing messaging apps that feel like cameras and act like social media platforms. It's almost like these three distinct things have merged into one another, both in form and function. The line between social networks and messaging apps is starting to blur as messaging platforms take on more and more features beyond simple communication.

*"A quarter of all downloaded apps are abandoned after a single use. Only instant messaging bucks the trend. Over 2.5 billion people have at least one messaging app installed. Within a couple of years, that will reach 3.6 billion, about half of humanity...Many teenagers now spend more time on smartphones sending instant messages than perusing social networks"*

-THE ECONOMIST[72]

Because Snapchat is a messaging-based app, the expectation is that users will talk to one another. As Snapchatters continue to share one-to-one or within groups, they are connecting at a deeper level with their community, and telling people who they are or who they hope to be. As we watch Stories, the subliminal command "chat" is always visible at the bottom of the screen (if that person's settings are public or you are friends). Snapchatters seem to be much more open to the idea of talking with people they haven't met than they are on other platforms. The magic of Snapchat is that it's a platform where people don't feel awkward about connecting with you. If I didn't know someone on Facebook, I'm not likely to send them a private message, yet with Snapchat, I don't feel like that. I already feel like I know them somehow, and we are part of a secret society that "gets it." It's an incredible conduit for individual outreach and connection.

- **Empathy**: We can't help connect with others to whom we relate. We see ourselves in their struggles and wins, which accelerates a bonding process.

Snapchat exploited our innate need to belong to a community, to become part of an inner circle of people who were like us and understood us.

■   ■   ■

## OUR BRAINS ON FACES

### Facial Recognition

Snapchat knowingly exploited neuroscience when they made an app all about showing our faces. Seeing someone face-to-face accelerates trust, which is one of the main reasons communities form so quickly within the app. As humans, we're hardwired to connect with faces and images more than text. When it comes to functionality, our brains and cameras have a lot in common. Just like the camera captures an image, so does a part of our brain called the Fusiform Gyrus[73]. This part of our brain is dedicated to identifying faces, a bio-skill that came in handy during our hunter-gatherer days. Back then, we needed to instantaneously identify friend from foe to avoid becoming dinner. Today, we use this part of our brains to connect with others and determine how to react in a social setting. Facial perception has always played a big role in our interpersonal interactions. Over 30 percent[74] of our brain is reserved just for visual processing, but the impressive part about this is that when we process visuals, our visual system involves over half[75] of our brain to finalize the processing, sending electrical impulses all over the place.

Recognizing a face is actually a very complex neural process and is extremely powerful in affecting our emotions. Even babies as young as

7 months old can tell a fearful face from a happy face[76]. Minutes after birth, infants seeking out parents faces and will begin to learn by copying the actions of our parents—first we see, then we do.

Scientists in the 1960s[77] suggested that we have neurons that respond only to specific faces, like your grandmother's face, for example. However, it wasn't until a study[78] conducted in 2005 by neuroscientist, Rodrigo Quian Quiroga, that the medical community started to pay attention to the idea of a "grandmother cell." Quiroga showed images of celebrities to epileptic patients while monitoring their brains. While showing a picture of Jennifer Aniston to patients, he found that only one specific neuron fired in their brains. Now, this isn't to say that we all have a Jennifer Aniston neuron. What these findings suggest is that our brains do, in fact, have specific neurons that only identify with one concept. Basically, faces are so important that our brains are fire in specific patterns when we look at specific people. Now, you can imagine how Snapchat ignites our brain cells by showing our community members' faces day after day.

## Mirror Neurons

We are born to mimic one another—we imitate each other's facial expressions, emotions, and actions. Small children learn how to walk, talk, and understand social cues based on watching their parents.

We also have special brain cells, called mirror neurons, which help us to understand how other people feel and how we should act in the presence of others, based on their facial expressions. It's what allows us to function as social beings. We use these parts of our brain to navigate interactions with others and make sense of the small nuances of body language.

Mirror neurons[79] explain the emotional rollercoaster we experience watching the final game of the season, or why when we see someone crying in a movie, we may be moved to cry as well, even though we know it's only a movie. When we see someone smiling, our own neurons start to react, firing as if we were actually smiling ourselves. It's why laughing is contagious and why Debbie Downers make us irritable. We don't even have to be doing the action ourselves to activate those brain cells! The simple act of watching another person run the ball down the field or imagining ourselves completing a touchdown causes every single muscle fiber and neuron to fire, as if we were actually on the field. So, when we watch our friends via Snapchat every day, we are experiencing their wins and losses with them. Observing others not only influences our behaviors but also facilitates a feeling of familiarity or relatability.

## Eye Contact

Emotional connection is heightened when we literally see eye-to-eye with someone. Eye contact communicates that you are focused on what the other party is saying, which is a key element to creating trust. In fact, looking someone directly in the eye can be such a sign of intimacy that we may avert our eyes when they accidentally meet a stranger's, across the room.

A Japanese study published in the journal, *Neuroimage*[80], paired 96 strangers together and instructed them to hold eye contact. Their findings showed that the same part of our brains responsible for facial recognition (Fusiform Gyrus), was at it again. The researchers noted that the activity in this brain region indicated that eye contact resulted in "eye-blink synchronization, which is believed to be a behavioral index of shared attention," or, in other words, when you're making eye contact, your brain's neurons are literally in sync.

When we Snap or watch other Snapchatters, we are seeing each other eye to eye, and that accelerates trust.

## Emoji-tions

Believe it or not, our love affair with faces is why emojis became a thing. The word "emoji" comes from the Japanese words for e (picture) + moji (character). Cute little faces and images are an easier, more emotion packed way for us to communicate than text alone. Emojis add a layer of context to our communication—admit it, if you don't get an emoji in a text message, you start to wonder, "Is he/she mad at me?" Over 92[81] percent of the internet population uses emojis, both men and women, young and old. Nearly three quarters of the U.S. population are using emojis on the regular, sending upwards of 96[82] per day on average.

Why do we care? Because emojis are more than just an adorable cartoon. Our brains are interpreting these images as nonverbal cues or emotions[83]. Even science has backed up this phenomenon in recent studies, which show that our brains react to emojis the same way as if we see someone LOL in real life.

In 2016, Snapchat purchased Bitmoji, a company that allows you to create your very own personal avatar (cartoon) that looks just like you, because they understood that emoji are an important part of expressing emotion via text messaging. Even the Oxford Dictionary[84] announced "emoji" as their word of the year in 2015 ("lumbersexual" and "on fleek" also made the short list).

The science of Snapchat doesn't need any further explanation than this: because we're looking at people's faces the majority of the time while Snapchatting, our brains love it. And because our brains love it, we keep coming back to the app and feel drawn to the face-to-face communication.

Snapchat gives good face.

■　　■　　■

## TOYS, GAMES, AND CREATIVITY

Snapchat was intended to be fun and toy-like. Toys and games don't need an explanation as to why children want to play with them— they're just plain fun. Toys are also incredible vehicles for learning, which is why parents love to buy fun toys that also offer an educational component. Legos teach us fine motor skills and how to visualize and follow complex directions. Toys teach children's brains to be imaginative in ways that benefit neural growth and form social development.

Snapchat encouraged users to express themselves creatively. The photos and videos themselves are only half the fun of Snapchat—it's the funny comments, memes, and hilarious filters that we use to enhance them that really make users love using it.

## Mastery

If you ever played Nintendo, you likely played The Legend of Zelda or Mike Tyson's Punch-Out!!. If you did, you probably remember the rush of getting to a new level. When I was a kid, I remember telling myself that I would save my game and turn it off once I got to the next level, but when I got there I couldn't help exploring it. Even if you've never played these games, you can relate to the feeling of accomplishment in mastering something new. Just like figuring out a new game, Snapchat was kind of difficult to maneuver and wasn't intuitive to most "mature" users. Once we mastered it, we were more likely to continue using it (like the Investment portion of the Hook Model). Unlike a lego set, Snapchat didn't come with directions, and that's why most people gave up on it. Similarly, because Snapchat was intended to be fun and toy-like, there was a certain level of gamification and mastery that served as catalyst for habit-formation.

Snapchat also included these game-like elements within the app:

- **Trophy Case:** Snapchat rewards users each time they achieve a milestone or complete a specific action. Snapchat does not tell users how to unlock them, which encourages exploration.

- **Snapchat Friend Emoji:** Snapchat monitors your messaging habits with friends and assigns emojis based on your level of interaction. This encourages users to communicate regularly, and provides a unique metric of interaction amongst friends.
- **Streaks:** A streak occurs when two people message each other every day without a break. Many users use this as a game and don't want to lose their "streakscore." Some users even feel anxiety or a compulsion to make sure they continue the game.

## Creativity

Snapchat was one of the first social apps that included a creative suite of tools that allowed users to communicate without saying a word. We could swipe to add a filter, type in text, and even create our own Stickers from images. The Lenses and Geofilters are artistic ways to enhance your content and express yourself in a more visual manner. Even the advertising was creative and interactive. It is, perhaps, one of the only types of ads that consumers WANTED to engage with. Art is a creative outlet for many of us and brings us back to enjoyable memories from our childhood, as well.

> *"We built our business on creativity and we're going to have to go through an education process for the next five years to explain to people how our users and that creativity creates value[85]."*

> Evan Spiegel, CEO Snap Inc.

Snapchat made us more creatively resourceful. When Snapchat first debuted, its artistic elements weren't nearly as advanced as today's version. The lack of options actually resulted more user creativity. As they say, necessity is the mother of all invention, which meant that learning to work with what we had was key. There are even some Snapchatters who use the medium to create micro-cinematic "films" while others have made a name for themselves creating art with its drawing tools.

Snapchat artists have amassed media attention and throngs of viewers who want to see their latest creations or participate in their contests.

Snapchat was a real piece of work—artwork, that is.

■ ■ ■

## SOCIAL MEDIA XANAX

### Under Pressure

Prior to Snapchat, social media images weren't typically raw and unedited. We felt like we had to share the best representations of ourselves, because that's what everyone else did. When I was a kid, I loved taking pictures that were fun and silly, but as an adult, I only wanted to post pictures that made me look my personal best. Pics were posted ONLY after they were filtered within an inch of their life, and of course, the angles had to be just right.

Posting to Instagram was stressful for me. Making sure that I was using the same color scheme or filters to make my feed look like a cohesive curated collection required me to use some brainpower. It wasn't spontaneous or fun. I once Googled "Instagram feed themes," and there were over 2 million results with titles like, "How to Make Your Instagram Feed Perfect" and, "The Complete Guide to Crafting a Beautiful Instagram Feed." The pressure was unreal—why did I have to make my Instafeed look perfect? Wasn't being myself enough?

I was suffering from Perfect Image Syndrome.

Snapchat offered a no-stress environment. Unlike other platforms, your photos and videos weren't stored forever in a timeline. People were choosing to move from the curated public eye to the private forums of "dark" social. Not dark in the sinister sense, but the kind of environment where people felt safe to share their real selves—no makeup, goofy faces, and the like. The pressure to craft a "like-worthy" image didn't exist.

Snapchat was relaxing and fun. So what if I took a pic of me with crazy bedhead? It would just disappear. I didn't feel the need to create perfected images that correlated to surrounding grid or gallery. There weren't any rules and I loved it. In fact, it seemed like I was actually rewarded for being real by my community—I was relatable and not afraid to embrace my quirkiness. While Snapchat does offer some exceptionally flattering filters that can easily Photoshop your selfie, users generally don't feel the same pressures in this private and mostly ephemeral environment.

Snapchat made me fall in love with the camera all over again.

**Snapchat eliminates "vanity metrics":**

- No public follower or friend counts
- No way to view who is following whom
- No public view count, comments, or "likes"

Snapchat encouraged engagement over metrics, maniacally focusing on creating a user experience that would be intrinsically rewarding. Limited and private metrics created a level playing field for all users—whether you were a famous celebrity or a middle-aged mom, no one could see how many followers you had or the number of likes received. You decided if someone you watched was "popular" based solely on your own opinion, not outside influences. If you liked their content then you continued watching and if you didn't like it, you skipped it. Freeing ourselves from a public value system of likes, reactions, and retweets created a completely stress-free environment that users loved. We can all agree that metrics do provide feedback of how your brand and core message is resonating with your audience, however, in my opinion, the true measure for any social platform is the quality of the conversations that you have within your community.

■　　■　　■

## INTENTIONAL ENGAGEMENT

One of the major complaints about Snapchat is lack of discoverability. You can't import your friends list or type in someone's first and last name to find them within the app. Unless your contact information is already saved in my phone, I have a screenshot of your Snapcode, or know your exact username (which is often not someone's first and last name), I can't find you. By design, Snapchat knew the value of a small, but highly engaged, community. They wanted people to connect with others like we do in real life. Friends introduce us to others, or we meet people at networking groups. It's a one by one process, not a meeting-hundreds-of-people-a-day process.

Snapchat is an app powered by interaction, not just passive viewing. Yes, there are lurkers who only watch and never comment or engage, but the majority of users are taking advantage of the messaging capabilities to talk with people. Snapchat maintains the highest user engagement levels of any other messaging or social platform to date, with 60 percent[86] of users creating content on a daily basis. When you are Snapping, you have to hold the button—that requires intention and attention. Before you can access the chat or stories screens of the app you have to physically decide to take an action and swipe left or right. I know it seems trivial, it's only one little swipe, but it goes much deeper that a quick flick of the finger.

The number one reason people love Snapchat: users choose whom they follow and what they see, in an algorithm-free environment.

Snapchat gives users control by allowing them to choose their content and their friends. Simultaneously, limiting the discoverability of other users forced us to get really intentional about who our community was.

Facebook and Instagram content is sorted by their proprietary algorithms based on an unknown amount of variables. Some of them may be based on your relationship to the person posting, if you recently engaged with their content, or what actions you've taken on the platform, like clicking a link or watching a video. Basically, these platforms are serving users what they think they will want to see the most, or what may be the most relevant. I don't get to pick and choose what I see in my Feed, that's been done for me based on previous behaviors on the platform.

Snapchat encouraged users to be really intentional, not only with whom they connected, but also in the way they consumed content—the user was in control, not a mathematical formula that decided what you should see. By design, the app's creators didn't want to create an oversaturated feed of random noise that would overwhelm users. By not creating a directory or easy search to find other users, Snapchat ensured that users would connect with purpose and create a community by choice.

By Design:

- No algorithm determining which content is shown.
- No Auto-Play feature—Users actively and intentionally must select your Story to watch it.
- No mass Snap send feature (thank goodness!).
- No "social drive-bys," or simply tapping a "like" button— Clicking a quick thumbs up on a Facebook post is sort of the lazy man's way to say hello, whereas in Snapchat you actually have to swipe up and type something in to chat.
- Limited discoverability – To find another Snapchatter, must know username, phone number or have Snapcode.

When we scroll through the feeds of other social platforms, we're passively taking in content that we've taught the algorithms to serve us. With Snapchat, I choose whom I watch by actively selecting those people's stories. It's not just a never ending feed of content served up to me by an algorithm. I know that algorithms think they know me pretty well, but I know myself better.

Snapchat put the user in control by allowing them to choose who would receive their messages. When posting on Facebook or Tweeting out a comment in the Twittersphere, we have no way of knowing exactly who sees that content, unless they take an action such as liking, commenting, or retweeting. No one can view your Snapchat without your express permission.

With Snapchat, we're tasked with creating content immediately, not passively viewing other people's content. Now, we open up Snapchat and select which friend's episode we want to watch. I don't have to scroll through thousands of posts before I find the latest update from the people I want to check in on.

Snapchat gives you control.

Part 3
The Snapchat Brand Building Formula

# 9

## Build A Powerful Personal Brand

*"Plain and simple, Snapchat helps you tell Stories, face to face, anytime, anywhere for free."*

*- Chelsea*

### OLD SCHOOL PHILOSOPHY FOR NEW SCHOOL MEDIA

Back in the old days (also known as the 90s), brands orchestrated consumer perception with glossy campaigns and memorable taglines. Now, nearly half of the United States is using ad blocking software[87], which means that traditional interruption marketing (commercials and banner ads) is now ignored. Those nuisances have become background noise, like the incessant yammering of kids in the back of the car, easily drowned out by parents who've become accustomed to the sound.

We want authentic conversations, not pre-packaged brochures that highlight a brand's award-winning product or service. Today's empowered consumer nimbly tweets a 140 character review in real time or Yelps your reputation into the ground. We share our good and bad experiences with hundreds, if not thousands, of people in less than two clicks. Because of this, brands no longer have the luxury of representing themselves as anything other than transparent. We want our voices to be heard, and we won't tolerate the wool being pulled over our eyes. In order to stay relevant and create loyal fans, today's brands must use social media in a much different manner than the traditional sales and marketing pitch platforms. The brand strategy needs to focus on how a brand can integrate into their ideal consumer's community and engage them in meaningful conversations. Brands that win talk with their audience, listen to what their needs are, and then create an experience that meets and, ideally, exceeds those needs.

It's about communication, not commercials.

When most people think of a brand, they think of behemoth companies like Nike or Apple—recognizable entities with brain-staining logos. A brand is not a logo. A brand is an intangible feeling that creates a consumer expectation. I believe branding is more accurately defined as a collection of shared experiences that take place over time, compounding until they create a short cut in someone's mind. The ultimate goal of every brand is to become associated with a consumer's need so much so that when someone thinks of "x," they almost unconsciously think of your brand. This requires earning consumer trust. Trust is a slow play—you can't rush it, fake it, or manufacture it because we are all too savvy to be sold. A company can hire a marketing agency to strategically craft a message that portrays an idealized version of their product or service, but the consumer will always confirm if that message is accurate. Building trust requires consistently meeting consumer expectations and delivering value without obligation.

As Amazon founder, Jeff Bezos, said, "Your brand is what people say about you when you're not in the room[88]." Each and every one of us has a brand that we've created with or without intention. Try as we might, we can't hide completely from the "always on" internet world and, if you're participating on social media, radio, TV, or any publishing or broadcast platform, you have a brand, and more importantly, a very public one. Whether or not you plan to use Snapchat (or any platform) for business, it's important to consider your public image.

In today's peer-to-peer economy, we depend on the experiences of others to help us make our own decisions. It's a psychological phenomenon known as Social Proof. At the most basic level, it means that we value the wisdom of the group. We tend to think that collective wisdom outweighs the individual. The more we see other people giving their approval, the more likely we are to do so. This is why Amazon, Uber, and everything in between uses a star-rating system. Social proof is so powerful that we may not trust someone unless we can review their social profiles. We want to see if we share friends in common and if they seem well-liked. We start to get concerned when we come across someone without any social presence. Do they have something to hide? Are they a serial killer? Nothing is more unsettling today than a social media ghost. According to CareerBuilder research[89], over 60 percent of employers are checking out social sites at some point in the review process and more than 41 percent said they were less likely to interview someone for a job if they couldn't find information about them online.

We've always trusted recommendations, but now we look to people outside of our immediate family or social circles for advice. This is called influencer marketing, and it has become a multi-billion dollar economy. When I was a kid, becoming "internet famous" wasn't a respected or lucrative career choice—heck, that option didn't even exist. Now, kids dream about becoming a globally known YouTuber or making big bucks posting photos to Instagram. According to MuseFind[90], "92% of Millennials trust a social media influencer more than the most famous celebrity." This kind of marketing isn't new. Remember the Wheaties boxes with famous athletes' faces on the front? How 'bout actresses posing for full page makeup ads in magazines? Influencer marketing is just a modern day celebrity endorsement. While typically more subtle than traditional advertisements, influencers will often review a product or place it strategically within their social posts, giving a personal endorsement whether implied or stated.

The reason that these people can actually influence is *because* of their personal brand. They've built up loyalty and trust within their community. Through the power of real time visual platforms, influencers can communicate with their community on a more personal level. Every day, their brand is present and consistent in providing value specific to the needs of their audience, which creates deep consumer loyalty. Not only do consumers feel like they know the influencer, but they also feel that their endorsements are more organic than an obvious advertisement. This kind of marketing demonstrates how brand trust leads to influence.

### Value + Trust = Influence

The most valuable influencer marketing campaigns are the ones that "seem" the most organic, which is why I personally believe that the soloprenuers and small businesses have an advantage over larger corporations because we can easily share our authentic stories. Top marketers understand the power of a personal brand because they know that at the end of the day, people buy *people*, not just the product. I'm not suggesting that you have to become an influencer or work with one to build a powerful personal brand. My point is this: branding today is about earned trust through community building, organic communication, and authenticity.

Remember, if you don't define your brand, someone else will.

■　　■　　■

## THE FOUNDATION OF YOUR BRAND
Understanding what a brand is and why you need to have one is only the beginning. The hardest part of branding is the "how." This process

requires dedication, a long-term commitment, and an understanding that building your brand isn't nearly as important as maintaining it. The first steps should focus on identifying your target audience, defining your message, and creating a content strategy that aligns with your message.

## 1. **Define a Niche to Become Known**

Becoming an established authority in a smaller niche can give you the credibility that you need to help your brand become known and compete with larger companies. It may sound counter-intuitive to narrow your audience to a small or very specific segment. However, when you know exactly who you are speaking to, you know exactly what kind of stories to tell. In turn, your audience will know what to expect from your channel. As humans, we like predictability—it is a necessary component of the trust building process. Every time your brand shows up and delivers value and meets a consumer expectation, one more building block of trust is laid in the foundation. This ongoing process requires consistent content creation and audience targeting. When you become a thought leader and resource for your community, people will seek out your advice, service or product to solve a problem because they trust you.

Benefits of a niche:

- If you are extremely specific with your audience you will know what their passions and interests are, which will enable you to craft content that will resonate.
- When you focus on one theme or topic, you become a reliable resource of content and expertise within that niche. In turn, your audience will be able to provide you with better, more qualified referrals for your business.
- The smaller the community size, the greater opportunity for influence. Most people who are interested in a niche are typically passionate about that subject and will have immediate

commonalities with other community members and develop a deep loyalty to your brand.

- The majority of consumers would rather work with someone who is known (or perceived) as a niche specialist than with someone who has a large company or a recognizable logo, but may be perceived as a generalist. We value highly personalized service executed by a true expert.
- When you're focused on a small community, you can create higher quality relationships because you are engaging with fewer people on a more intimate level. It's not the number of followers or fans that you have, it's how engaged they are. I think most of us can agree that having a huge following with thousands of people who never convert to a sale or engage with you in any meaningful manner isn't as valuable as a small but highly engaged tribe of loyalists.
- Future branding and marketing decisions are much easier when you are working with a niche—it either aligns with your niche or it doesn't.

Typically, people seek out a niche that will align with their passions or they believe will make them money. If you can do both, even better. If you're only looking to make money, I would suggest, at the very least, that you have some level of interest in the subject. There are some fields about which you can learn almost everything, however, most industries continue to evolve, which requires a commitment to continuing education. You don't have to be THE expert to build authority in a niche. You can become AN expert over time and, to be honest, I find it refreshing when someone that I view as an expert continues to advance their personal knowledge and shares that experience with their community. It's nice to know that experts are human too—they don't have to know it all, they just have to know enough to inspire, educate, and guide.

It doesn't matter what you are known for, it only matters that you are known. People may not remember your company name or where exactly you live, but if you are consistent with your message and you provide value through education or entertainment (even if you are controversial), people will remember that you are the person who's the "Fill-in-the-blank" person. If you love baking cookies, and you share that passion consistently, and people can experience your amazing creations, then you become the "Cookie Person." If you love red wines and you review them on your channel and take viewers on tours of local vineyards, then you become the "Red Wine Person."

How do you want to be known?

## 2. **Develop a Core Message**

If you're not clear about what your brand represents, no one else will be, either. I see too many entrepreneurs trying to be everything to everyone, which is a short term plan. Eventually, you have to pick a lane. If you tell consumers that you do it all, they start to feel like you're dishonest, or think that you can't possibly do everything well, so your quality must not be up to snuff.

This is why creating one core message for your brand is critical. Some people might call this your "unique value proposition" or "mission statement." A core message can be as simple as describing what you love to do, how you help people, or a catch phrase or tagline. This doesn't mean that you have to repeat one sentence, tagline, or intro every single time you are using Snapchat, but it does mean that your content should reflect a consistent, singular focus around one passion, industry, or subject matter. Without repetition, your target audience won't be able to easily build those mental shortcuts.

The key to creating a memorable core message is making it very easy to understand. A core message should succinctly communicate in one to two sentences what you do, and why it benefits your niche audience. It's not about features, it's about the benefits. Features are about the product or service, and benefits are about the customer. It doesn't include industry jargon or complex concepts. The most beloved brands can explain their value proposition in plain language. Can you describe what you do and how it helps people simply enough that a six-year-old could understand it? Can they repeat it back to you? When you see professional speakers on stages that move or inspire a crowd, it's typically because they can talk about their topic, articulately. Not only do they know the topic forwards and backwards, but they can also explain it in a way that feels fresh and passionate, rather than relying on rote memorization. They are very clear on what they do and why it's important. The only way this kind of mastery and confidence happens is when you truly understand your "why" and have become a practitioner with firsthand experience. It's also important to be very specific about why you are uniquely positioned as the expert in your niche. What makes you different than others in your field?

It's critical to consider the *tone* of your message. Is it lighthearted, funny, serious, or uplifting? If you're naturally funny, then injecting this into your brand makes sense, and your content message would include this kind of tone. If you're in a serious role, it may not make sense. Think about your topic and whom you are trying to reach, and if the tone that you are using is appropriate.

Now that you know who you're talking to and what to say, let's talk about how to deliver your message in an impactful way.

### 3. Create Value Through Content

Content marketing. If you're a marketer or plan to be, you'll hear this term constantly. Content marketing is defined as:

> *"A strategic marketing approach focused on creating and distributing valuable, relevant, and consistent content to attract and retain a clearly defined audience—and, ultimately, to drive profitable customer action[91]."*

> - CONTENT MARKETING INSTITUTE

We won't review this again, but basically, content is made to help people, not sell them and position yourself as someone who knows what they're doing.

The value proposition of Snapchat has little to do with voice-changing, bunny-faced video Lenses. Its value is helping you to communicate in the most powerful format (real time video) for free, at any time. The number one thing that consumers want from any brand is authenticity and honesty. The most direct way to build trust is to talk to people directly, face to face.

Thanks to apps like Snapchat, the phone has been completely transformed into a free branding platform with a built in broadcast network that's always with us. Tomorrow's consumer is absolutely going to expect us to have our own television channels, where we are the stars of the show. Being the star of your own show isn't about ego or fame, it's about connecting with people in the MOST human way possible.

Snapchat was the first mobile messaging app that allowed us to communicate screen-to-screen at a literal arm's length, showing our faces and sharing our stories. It's the closest thing to being in real life without actually being in the same physical space.

I have a confession. I don't watch TV anymore because it doesn't talk back, and neither will any generation after this one. Okay, that may have been a little extreme, or at the very least, a little premature. Yes, we will still watch "programmatic" content, but with Facebook and Snapchat launching their versions of Netflix-like entertainment, TV as we know it is going to change, big-time. We simply cannot build a powerful personal brand in 2018 world without using the camera.

Building a camera-first brand makes perfect sense because of these three things:

1. Video appeals to every demographic – whether you're 8 or 80, we all love watching video.
2. Our brains are physically wired to connect with faces. We have a special part of our brains dedicated only to facial recognition, and when you can see someone every day, eye-to-eye and can talk with them directly, you become relatable. When you're relatable, you become very relevant.
3. We're spending several hours a day using our phones to consume digital media. The camera is mobile and always with us. There's no barrier to entry, and no gatekeepers keeping you from reaching your target audience and sharing your stories at scale. It's easy to make content with Snapchat—there's no software, no downloading or uploading, and no third party editing tools needed. Pulling out your phone and Snapping a few minutes of content a day is a lot more practical and efficient than more traditional forms of content creation, like blogging or writing a book (ahem).

***Real time visual communication is a fundamental shift in how we're going to be connecting with consumers and sharing our brand.***

■  ■  ■

## CREATING CONTENT THAT CONNECTS

### Storytelling Not Storyselling

"Storytelling" is a marketing buzzword we read in the headlines of countless marketing blogs. We get it—be authentic, be real, and then film it. Snapchat loves stories (and so do we). It's one of the reasons they opted to name their feature "Stories" and why they make users' content appear in chronological order, because they understand that every good story has a beginning, a middle, and an end. They also know that the best stories are the ones we create just living our daily lives. Our personal narrative is perhaps the only thing we can ever actually share at scale, because it's always with us and we're the ones who know it best[92]. There's no keyword research or algorithm hacks required when you're documenting your personal experiences. Creating content that helps, educates, or inspires your niche is a requirement. Real time authentic stories that invite your niche to participate within the narrative while connecting them to a larger community is ideal.

Here are some reasons that storytelling isn't merely a marketing term du jour:

- **It skips the selling**: When you're telling a story, you're not selling anything, which means that there are no sales objections to overcome. People don't feel like you're being pushy, they just feel like you're being you. If your goal is to generate business using Snapchat, you can't get conversions without conversations.
- **It shows them**: People want you to *show* them who you are, not tell them—that's what Gary Vaynerchuk meant when he said to start documenting the "behind the scenes" of your daily life. People will naturally see what you do without you ever having to sell them your services. This allows your expertise to shine through without pushing a brochure in their faces about why you're the best. It also allows the consumer to decide if your brand is authentic. It's vital that you are a practitioner—people want to see that you walk the walk, and not just talk the talk.
- **It invites them in**: When you take people on a journey with you, they become invested. Just like watching a dramatic or suspenseful movie, we find ourselves wanting to see what happens next. We want to see people overcome challenges and achieve goals. Snapchat allows you to invite your audience into your life in an intimate way. Your audience is with you as you begin your journey, and when you end it. When we watch

others' Stories, it makes us feel good because we believe, even in the smallest way, that we had a part in their win.

- **It starts a conversation**: Most importantly, Snapchat enables your story to become a two-way conversation. Snapchat, at its core, is a messaging app that encourages communication. Talking is *personal*. Talking builds rapport, and rapport builds trust. Engagement is the Holy Grail metric in today's marketing.
- **It makes you relatable**: People can see themselves in your story and that helps you build the #1 thing that you need as a brand. *The most underleveraged marketing tactic today is relatability and relatability <u>explodes</u> when we're vulnerable on camera.*

**People want stories, not sales pitches.**

## Consistency

When you only focus on one thing and deliver CONSISTENTLY, you become synonymous with the word "specialist," and that's when you become known. Think about Target stores—they all look the same, by design. We can travel to any other state and walk into a Target and feel like home. They're consistent. They want people to feel like they are coming to a place where they know where things are. It's not just about design or set up, it's also about how often your brand shows up and delivers. If you think about someone whom you know that you can call on at any time and they have your back, those are the people who have been consistent. They're reliable. They're your ride or die. Consistency builds trust.

Your brand will need to commit to creating content and telling stories on a consistent basis. Due to the nature of Snapchat and its short-lived format, creating content consistently throughout the day is an important strategy. Since the Stories feed is in chronological order, at the time of this book's publishing, Snapping regularly will push your Story closer to the top of the Feed. The only way to "game" the system is by adding snaps to your story on a regular basis so you show up at the top of your friends Story feed. However, creating low value Snaps will quickly encourage viewers to skip past your Stories. In other words, attempting to game the system by Snapping all the time may not be the best strategy for growing an authentic and valuable personal brand.

## Context is King

Your content doesn't have to fit into a restrictive box. It doesn't have to be a checklist, a whitepaper, or a tutorial to bring value to your audience. The secret sauce for content is making it connect with your audience, and that's where context comes into play. The content is your actual message, and the *context* is how you give meaning to your message. It's how you make your stories connect with people's heads and hearts. Context is providing the right message, at the right time, to the right people. It's not only about the content itself, but also how we experience that content makes us feel. Context is like an algorithm for VALUE. It helps you get seen more by the people who matter to your business. Because Snapchat is a camera first and a social network second, it's visual, and that adds a unique element of context to your stories by default.

Here are five ways to create context:

## The 5 E's of Context

1. **Educate**: Teach your audience something new. You're valuable if your message makes someone feel more informed or better prepared to make a decision.
2. **Entertain**: Make them laugh or think of something in a new or different way.

3. **Emotions**: Make them feel something. Inspire or motivate them. Be vulnerable and share your story.
4. **Exclusive**: Make them an insider. Deliver content they can only see on your Snapchat channel.
5. **Engage**: Make THEM matter. Commenting on their Stories makes your community feel heard. Asking them questions invites them into a shared story.

■ ■ ■

# 10

## Start Snapping

*"Don't compare your beginning to someone else's middle."*

— TIM HILLER, AUTHOR

### GET OVER YOURSELF

The first time I saw myself on camera was horrifying. Did my voice really sound like that in person? Why hadn't anyone told me about my semi-crossed left eye before? How often did I say "um" in the span of three minutes? What if no one watched my Snaps? Or worse—what if someone did watch?

These might be the same questions rumbling around in your head right now—that voice, it's called fear. We often compare ourselves to others (thanks in part to social media), and can be our own worst critics. Let me ask you this: when you're watching someone else's video content, are you constantly critiquing their appearance or voice? For the most part, I'm sure your answer is "no." Yet, we allow the opinions of others, perceived or real, to prevent us from sharing our unique talents with the world. The good news is that you're not alone in this fear. The bad news is if you don't quiet those irrational voices, you'll never be able to share your story that could be the very content someone is waiting to hear. Self-confidence and self-esteem go hand in hand. Luckily, both can be learned.

I am a perfectionist by nature. Prior to using Snapchat, I had dabbled in live streaming, used Periscope for a hot minute and then Facebook Live. I was so uncomfortable watching myself on camera that I vowed to not watch any of my own content back for an entire year. What I learned from this avoidance strategy was that I completely hamstrung the speed of my own progress. If I had watched myself back and asked others for feedback, I would have felt a little like a loser for a while, maybe a bit embarrassed, but I would have improved my camera presence in half the time. I knew that if I was going to become a true practitioner, I would have to get over myself. Getting over the idea that everything had to be perfect in order to be valuable to an audience was the best thing I ever did.

Being yourself is perhaps the biggest challenge you will face during this process. Sharing our quirks, fears, failures, and wins can make us feel vulnerable, which sets off those neurological fire alarms designed to protect us. Our brains always recall negative experiences faster and more vividly than positive ones, which is a built in evolutionary protection mechanism. As hunter-gatherers, we needed to learn quickly from our mistakes.

Our brains store negative crap for years.

> Look, Snapchat offers THE best Photoshopping around, so if you can't get over yourself here, I don't know where that will happen. Just use it and have fun with it. You WILL develop a level of comfort talking into the camera! Worst case scenario, you can delete anything you don't absolutely love!

Keep in mind, not everyone is going to be "a natural" on camera, and we all start at the beginning when we learn a new platform regardless of our innate talents. Many people tell me they plan to wait to create content until they can improve their camera presence or prepare talking points. What I tell them is this: you cannot possibly get to quality without quantity. In the early days of developing your content strategy, you will create a lot of content that might be "meh" or even downright poor quality. By creating consistently, you will improve on your style, delivery and presence. Once you've gotten into your groove, you can shift your main focus to refining the quality.

You won't arrive at any destination standing still.

■    ■    ■

## GET REAL

The biggest mistake I made when I was started creating content on Snapchat was that I only talked about business. I was afraid if I wasn't giving educational content all the time, then I wasn't providing value. But then, one Sunday morning, my 4 year old son, Mason, got ahold of a black Sharpie marker and drew on every single white cabinet, wall, rug, pillow, and all over himself. I was so frustrated that I Snapped my #hotmessmom moment, and I got more engagement on that story than anything else I had ever done.

I was shocked because I didn't understand until that moment that value could exist beyond just talking about business all the time. I had an epiphany. Value isn't just a tip, a hack, or a coupon code. Value can be as simple as making someone laugh, or bonding over parenting fails. I realized that there is incredible value in CONNECTING with people in an authentic manner. Simply telling my story ignited my audience's memories of similar incidents that happened during their own parenting adventures. Remembering those moments triggered smiles and laughs and they immediately related to what it was like to be in a similar situation. Value comes in a lot of different shapes and sizes.

People want meaningful engagement that's real, not mass-market links and memes. Don't get me wrong, I love a good meme as much as the next person, but when confronted with "inspirationless"[*2] quotes, I scroll right past them. That's why the Chewbacca mask mom[93] went viral—it was an unplanned, unedited moment from a relatable mom. When I let my guard down, I let my audience in. For me, I found that poking fun of myself and my flaws allowed others to see that I wasn't hung up on being "perfect," and granted them the permission to laugh with me. When you begin your Snapchat journey, you're not going to be amazing. In fact, you may totally suck. I tend to see arcs in Snapchatting styles. Typically, new users are concerned about how they look and may overuse the Lenses because they give us something to hide behind—we feel safer, less exposed. Eventually, with practice, the Lenses often fall away and we accept who we are on camera. Vulnerability and authenticity go hand in hand and are responsible for how your audience will react to your content and how quickly they will fall in love with your brand.

I know what you're thinking,

**"But my life is boring, no one wants to see that."**

There can be magic in the mundane—it's where we really get to know people. Think about how we spend time talking with our families or co-workers. We're not always on an adventure or cracking jokes, we're just sharing our normal everyday happenings. Documenting what you know and are passionate about will provide value to someone. We want to know what happens, and we want to feel like we had a part in it.

Many people I speak with tell me that their lives are far too boring to document—that they don't know what to share and feel like people

---

2 *Inspirationless quotes were made Snapchat famous by @baierman11

would not be interested. They tell me that they don't really know how to be real through a mobile device and they don't have anything to talk about. Firstly, it's important to remember that many of the stories we tell ourselves are just that—stories. We try to talk ourselves out of trying new things out of a fear of the unknown, or we compare ourselves to people who we feel are incredibly talented, and psych ourselves out thinking that we couldn't possibly ever be as good as "they" are. We take for granted that what we do could help or inspire others. When I decided to write this book, I documented the entire process. I imagine there are very few people who watch my content that aspire to write a book. However, lots of people want to see how to make content or see the process of designing a book cover. Some of them don't care at all that I wrote a book, but they cared that I was stressed or doubting myself and sent me encouragement. I invited them into my journey and many of them came along for the ride. When I published this book, they published it with me.

If you're still unsure that you have anything interesting to share, I recommend watching some Stories for a while and if you find some people who are using Snapchat to educate or entertain or are within a profession you would like to be in, then emulate some of the content that they create. The simple act of talking into the camera and letting people know that you are trying to learn how to use Snapchat can give you content to talk about and makes you vulnerable which is very relatable to anyone who is…human.

It's important to remember not to minimize yourself. Statements like, "I'm just a" or "I'm only a" will hold you back. You may not think that you are different or unique, but everyone has their own opinions and experiences that make us totally one-of-a-kind. The beauty of being real is that your audience rewards you by sharing your brand with their community. They become the best marketing campaign you never paid for.

That's called loyalty.

## CHELSCHAT: MARKETING SNAPPILY EVER AFTER

*Because I am a marketer by trade, I tend to think about content in terms of a structured format like a blog or how-to video tutorial. When I began using Snapchat I naturally thought, "Oh, I'll make a daily show where I can give a new marketing tip each day." It seemed like the right thing to do based on my previous content experience.*

*I didn't use Snapchat to document in the beginning, I was purely creating. I'm telling you this because I want you to know that you can successfully build a brand and a community by only creating (however, I do believe that including personal content is key with this platform). I also want you to know that the kind of content that you start out with may not be where you end up, and that's okay, because it means that you are learning and adjusting to what works for you and your target audience.*

*I started by identifying my niche market: real estate professionals who wanted to learn how to use Snapchat to build their brand. That was a really narrow niche. By using an Excel spreadsheet, I planned out my content ideas and topics up to a month at a time. Then, every Monday through Friday, I Snapped about one tip that aligned with my core message. I created a simple, but memorable intro format that included a graphic made in Canva that I would record right from my computer screen with some music playing in the background on my Spotify app on my phone. In the next Snap, I dropped my Core Message:*

*"What's up everybody?! It's Chelschat Snapshow, Real Estate Marketing Snappily Ever After where I share tips, tools, and strategies that will help you grow your business and make more money doing what you love."*

*It was simple and told my specific audience what value they would get from watching my show. At that time, Snapchat limited all Snaps to*

*10 seconds in length which meant I had to learn to talk really, really fast. That mouthful resulted in a quirky fast intro that made me sound like a professional auctioneer. Who knew that my intro Snap would become "my thing?" People all over the world had fun with it and tried to repeat it word for word within the time limit. Now, I don't believe that you need to make a "show" or even have a formal intro like I did. At the time, I was just "doing." Now, that has become my trademark, so I continue to use it.*

*I Snapped images of my notebook with summary notes on the topics and takeaways and also layered text over my video Snaps to allow viewers to take screenshots to refer to later. I began to develop a strategy to promote my content and grow my niche audience (which I list later on in this chapter). I hosted my show without ever missing one day for over a year. I was consistent with my content creation and my commitment to my niche audience. To this day, I still host this Snapshow Monday thru Friday.*

■　　■　　■

## GET BETTER

Now that you've started using Snapchat, here are some tips that can help you level up your Snapchat content:

- **Look at Me**: Look at the camera at the top of the phone, not your own eyes in the screen. When we look into the camera, we appear to be looking eye to eye with our viewer, which amplifies trust. This is the #1 tip for any video platform—it feels a little weird at first, but it will make or break your video content (thank you @bizaaron).
- **Be Succinct**: Snapchat has extended the original 10-second limit on video and still image Snaps. Now, users can record up to six 10-second video clips at once that are automatically "stitched" together. Keep in mind, viewers want micro-content in short intervals. Long form vlogging is best suited for other

platforms like YouTube. Just because you can take up more time doesn't always mean you should. In my opinion, the very best thing Snapchat ever did was to restrict the time of content creation, because it forced users to be concise and to the point.

- **Verbal Ticks**: Avoid starting every sentence with the same word like "so," "alright," or "um," and notice the sound your mouth makes you start to speak (I call this the Snapchat Smack). Typically, we don't notice these things when we're having a conversation with someone else, but when we're on camera, they are amplified.

- **Face Lenses**: They sure are fun, but if you plan to use Snapchat for business (and even if you don't) constantly using the Lenses (especially the voice-changing options) can distract from your content and make it difficult to understand what you are saying. Remember, people are here to get to know the real you, don't be afraid to show them!

- **Repetitive Snaps**: Every brand has its "thing," and I encourage brands to create a memorable intro or style, however, keep in mind that if you want to retain an audience over a period of time, sharing the same content or same series of Snaps every day or multiple times in the same day may result in loss of attention.

- **Selfies**: Again, moderation is the key here. Keep in mind that viewers want to see you communicate with them, which means talking—still photos of your selfies are less interesting and don't offer nearly as much opportunity for meaningful conversation.

- **Show Your Face**: Viewers are here to get to know people, which means the majority of your content should be your face and in video format. Don't be afraid to share views or photos of your perspective, heck, that's why Snap made Spectacles, but it's important to include your face when talking to people.

- **Photo Timer**: When Snapping still images, consider reducing the timer setting to under 5 seconds unless the image features lengthy text (if people want to re-read something they can simply tap back).

*NOTE: I rarely recommend using the "infinity" setting on the timer (also known as the dreaded "Loop" feature). Occasionally, this setting can be useful for creative effect, but most of the time it annoys the heck out of your viewers.

- **Keep it Vertical**: As we've discussed, vertical is the new black—save the horizontal pics for another platform, or, if you must use this orientation, use it sparingly. We all love a good sunset pic, but science has already proven we're pretty lazy. Good gracious, don't make us move our wrists back and forth!
- **Get Creative**: Snapchat was meant to bring out our fun, creative sides. Using the creative features like stickers, Geofilters and the drawing tools to enhance your Story is part of the Snapchat way.
- **Watch Out**: Be aware of what's in the background, reflections, or your appearance—sometimes we overlook things because we're so focused on what we're saying that we may not realize we've captured something embarrassing in the background!
- **Set the Stage**. Consider prepping the viewer or "setting the stage" on your Snaps if you're going to be sharing personal or behind the scenes content. Let's say you're at a work party and your audience doesn't know any of your co-workers. It may help keep their interest if you share *why* each person you are Snapping at the party is interesting, or some fun facts about your office. It helps your viewers remain interested and engaged in a sea of unknown people.
- **Plan**: If you prefer to create content with a more formal structure (i.e. educational, how to), here are some tips to help you maximize your success:

o You may find it helpful to use a content calendar or some kind of tracking system to note your topics and bullet points. Some online options or apps are: *Trello.com*, Evernote app, or good old Excel.

o If you choose to tell a story or teach a concept, make sure it has a clear beginning, middle, and end. Be sure to plan enough time to complete the series of Snaps in the story—no one wants a cliffhanger! You might consider writing or typing out the storyline (I used post-it notes, cuz I'm old school like that).

o Create a consistent schedule—treat it like a TV show or vlog, and host at the same time of day or same day of week. Some Snapchatters have created theme days like #TechTuesdays or #ThankfulThursdays which can help you organize your content and gives your viewers a heads up on which days they may want to tune in on.

o Don't be afraid to review your Story and delete any Snaps that may not make sense. Also, check to see if all of the Snaps posted. Sometimes, one or two can accidentally drop off, and then it leaves your audience wondering what happened! Also, what we feel like has a good flow while we're Snapping it, may not make as much sense in the finish product. Take some time to review the flow of your Story.

o Crowdsourcing can be an incredibly helpful when creating content—ask your audience what they want to see. To increase engagement, ask questions—this also gives you an opportunity to feature (or shout out) those who answer. I recommend asking their permission or letting them know up front you will be sharing their codes and comments.

o Maximize the text function to incorporate more information without taking up more time. Remember, viewers want content in short intervals. Adding more details or data points in the text overlay of your videos can help you pack more into your Snap and appeals to those viewers who like to read over watching video. Adding text also draws attention and encourages viewers to screenshot your information to reference at a later time.

o   Consider creating exclusive content only on Snapchat which can help you grow and retain an audience that knows they will not be able to view your content elsewhere.

o   If you're stressed about coming up with content ideas, consider using a blog aggregator that allows you to save articles from your favorite blogs in specific categories. You can search for blogs by keyword and topic! You might get some great inspiration from the latest trends in your subject matter. I love using *Feedly.com*.

- **Change Angles**: If you're planning to talk in a series of Snaps, be sure to vary your angles every now and again to maintain visual interest. Additionally, peppering in photos amongst your video Snaps can be a nice transition for the viewer—don't be afraid to use both formats.
- **Volume/Sound**: Keep in mind, if you are naturally soft-spoken, it may be difficult for your audience to hear your Snaps. Often, we will forgive poor visual quality, but not poor audio quality. In turn, if you're Snaps are very loud, you might not be audible, or if background music transitions from low to very loud quite often, that could also affect viewership.
- **Movement**: If you're using a zoom or fast movements for the occasional effect, totally fine. However, if you're continuously using fast movement in every Snap, it can make it difficult for your viewer to watch (read: seasick).
- **Share Codes**: Sharing is caring, and it's also the #1 way to help a community grow. Always give your community a reason **_why_** they should add the person you are sharing. Let the person know that you've shared their code as well!

*NOTE: Keep in mind only one code is scannable at a time, so if you showcase multiple codes on one Snap, viewers won't be able to easily scan them all and will have to take multiple steps. Sometimes, Snapchat can be glitch and codes may not scan, which is why I try to not only include their code but also their username.

- **Spam**: Direct messages were intended for personal communication and shouldn't be abused with spammy sales pitches or uninvited Snaps. Sending mass Snaps is perceived as impersonal and, quite frankly, it's annoying—this is a personal platform, so don't abuse it. Asking for shout outs or to "Put Me On Your Snapchat" is outright offensive to those who are using the platform to create genuine relationships. If you are looking for hacks there are plenty of places online to find people who want to do that—go follow them.
- **Private Chats**: Sharing another Snapchatter's direct message conversations, images or screenshots without their permission could be considered a violation of their privacy and trust. When in doubt, ask first.

*Note: Snapchat will notify you if a screenshot is taken of your Snap or within a chat. Users are also able to press and hold on a photo or video within a private chat and save it to their camera roll. Great for potential Story collaborations, not so great if you don't want anyone saving your images.

- **Streaks**: A Snapchat specific game in which, "you and your friend have Snapped each other (not chatted) within 24 hours for more than three consecutive days[94]." Some users like to see how long they can keep their Snapstreaks going and increase their Snapscores with this method. The majority of people who like to participate in this style of game will make it clear. Don't assume people want to play. Ask them first, and don't send irrelevant Streak Snaps. (By the way, your Snapscore isn't relevant to building your brand or growing a community).

- **Custom Stories AKA Group Stories**: Snapchat has a feature called a "Custom Stories," which allows a user to create a group Story with an unlimited amount of participants. It's a fun way to collaborate with friends and makes creating community storytelling during a popular event easier, BUT adding loads of people to this group story without asking for permission or giving any context is often viewed as rude, and it clutters up people's feeds. Err on the side of caution and ask for permission before adding.

- **Story Length:** There's no one-size-fits-all answer to this. Snapchat was designed to give viewers a glimpse into your life in small, real time increments. It embraces the ultimate micro-moment mentality that we have adopted as a society. We're training generations to glance at their mobile device the very second there is down time—in line at the grocery checkout, or even at a red light. Because we crave content bursts, it's even more important to consider how you are developing your content strategy for today's quick-fire demands. We now have to not only consider creating compelling content, but also how to keep it to the point while creating a cohesive storyline.

  From a brand perspective, a Snaplytics report[95] shared research from a case study conducted across 500 different brands that determined 11 Snaps seemed to be the magic number to hold attention and completion. Many articles echo the suggestion for shorter Stories, however, I subscribe to the philosophy of making your Story as long as it needs to be. If you feel compelled to Snap every minute of every day, fine—do what feels right to you. If you have interesting content, people will watch, and vice versa. If people complain, they can stop watching.

- **Repurposing**: You can save your Snaps and Stories, download them to your phone, and upload them into other platforms.

While it does save time to repurpose your Snaps, keep in mind that some purists feel that original content should be created natively within each app to preserve the different nuances of each network. Also, visually, you can tell when content was created in one platform and shared to another.

Personally, I like to create content natively in each of the platforms, even though it takes much more time and effort to come up with different ideas on multiple platforms. If you choose this option, perhaps cycling your content will help you be more efficient. For example, if you create content for Snapchat about a specific topic that you post on Monday, you may want to use that theme on Tuesday within a different platform. Keep in mind that if you have followers that are connected with you on multiple platforms, they will see repeat content. Lastly, if you do decide to repurpose, understand that certain platforms may not support the same sizing. For example, if you post a Snap to your Instagram feed, it will get cropped, so don't place any text at the extreme top or bottom. You could use third party apps or editors, but that sounds like a lot of extra work to me.

You should make the choice as to what works best for your goals. If you feel that repurposing will be more efficient for you or if you have different audiences on different platforms, then give it a try.

- **Safety**: Snapping while driving falls under the category of distracted driving. Understand that this could be potentially life threatening and illegal.

*Note: In June 2017, Snapchat unveiled its location based world map, called Snap Map, which allows users to see their friends on a map and what's happening around the globe. It's also frighteningly accurate and will track your exact location. If you don't want people knowing your location, then turn on "Ghostmode" in your settings, or only share your location with specific friends.

- o Access Snap Map by pinching your fingers together on the home screen.
- o Tap on the gear icon in the top right corner and select the settings you prefer.
- **Illegal Activity**: Although Snapchat content may be short lived, it can be screenshotted or recorded with another device and can create a lasting impact. Consider the consequences before posting any illegal activity (or any *legal* activities or commentary that doesn't align with your brand or your employer standards).
- **Swearing**: Consider how your target audience would responding to swearing. Be cognizant of what you say and how others may receive it. Again, your channel, your choice.
- **Rants**: Yes, we all have them, and they can be funny or help us bond over shared frustrations, BUT if you're content is *always* negative, you may turn people off. We are entitled to our opinions and have freedom of speech, but I would urge any brand to be thoughtful in how they use that influence.
- **Trolls:** Inappropriate messages and photos are a reality on any social network. This is where your privacy settings come into play. While it's not 100% avoidable in every case, here are my tips on how to determine if someone may be a troll, and how to proceed:
  - o If the person's Snapcode has no photo or Bitmoji, proceed with caution.
  - o If their username is obscene or contains foul language, this is usually a warning sign.
  - o If you receive a red message (photo) or a purple message (video) from someone you don't know, or if you have

recently added someone and they immediately send you one of these message formats, proceed with caution.

(To all of the normal, nice people who are sending heart-felt video welcome messages, please note that many users [including myself] will not open a video message if they do not already know you. Consider sending a voice message instead.)

o   If you receive an unwelcome message, you can block that person by pressing and holding on their name, tapping the gear icon, and selecting "Block." A pop up will appear and ask you the reason for blocking and you can select which-ever option you feel is appropriate.

o   You should know that if you receive an inappropriate mes-sage, it is not your fault. Troll behavior is much easier on social networks because it offers a level of anonymity, and quite simply, these people do it because they can.

- **Stop apologizing**: Not everyone will like your content, and that's what you want, whether you know it yet or not. You're brand and content should be focused on a primary target audi-ence or niche for maximum effectiveness. You can't be every-thing to everyone, and when you become very clear about what your core message is and who you want to receive it, your decisions about what your content will include, and how you will create and curate it will become second nature. Unusual clarity brings with it freedom. Keep in mind, anything that you put out into the universe, even if it's on a platform that is much more private than others, opens you up to public opinion and not everyone will like you or say nice things to you—the end.

# 11

## Discoverability

### GET FOUND

At the time of this book's publication, Snapchat offers limited discovery. In the beginning, there was zero discoverability. You had to know someone's username or have their Snapcode to find them. Snapchat limited discovery for a reason. They wanted us to be intentionally create real relationships as we would in real life. Snapchat is an intimate setting, which allows people to feel comfortable communicating, sharing, and getting to know people in an authentic way. We don't go out to the mall or coffee shop and meet a thousand people at once. We're introduced to others at parties or networking events and we get to know each other for a while. I do believe at some point Snapchat will likely improve discoverability, and at that time, they may have to start using an algorithm as well. No one can predict if or when this may ever happen.

Here are some suggestions on how to discover new Snapchatters and get discovered:

- **Add your phone contacts**: Anyone who is in your phone's contact list that has an account will appear. You can add any or all of those accounts.

- **Turn on "Add Nearby" setting**: Add people nearby who also have this setting turned on. Usually good for large events like conferences.
- **Review Snapcode directory websites**: Ghostcodes.com and Snapdex.com are online directories of Snapchatters' codes and a description of their Snapchannel content. While using a third party directory like Ghostcodes.com can help you selectively add people who share your same interests, it also doesn't prevent people from adding everyone in that directory without any rhyme or reason. Filling up your feed with a bunch of people who may just add you, and later on delete your account isn't generating a high ROI relationship.
- **Join groups on other social networks about Snapchat**: Search for Snapchat-specific groups and add members.
- **Wear your Snapcode**: Literally, put your code on hats or shirts. I'm stopped every time I wear my Snapcode shirt. I've seen many users create custom stickers as well (you may want to make sure you're not violating any public ordinances if you're thinking about plastering those stickers all over town, just sayin').
- **Market your Snapcode**: Include your code or username on your marketing materials, business cards, websites, social networks, and emails.
- **Read blogs**: You can easily find articles written that suggest Snapchatters to follow.
- **Join a Twitter Chat**: A Twitter chat is a public conversation that happens on Twitter that follows a specific hashtag. It typically has a topic and is scheduled on a regular basis. I highly recommend #ChatSnap, the Twitter Chat all about Snapchat created by @krisgillentine. Kristy created the first and only Twitter Chat for the SnapChat community attracting hundreds of weekly participants.

- **Ask other Snapchatters**: If you love watching someone's channel, ask them to share some of their favorite friends.
- **Play games**: Participate in Snapchatters' games on their channels. For example, some channels may have a weekly theme day where they ask their audience to send in snaps based on that theme and include their personal Snapcode so others can add them.
- **Shameless plug**: Add every one of the Snapchatters I list at the end of this book. You can thank me later.
- **Custom (group) Stories**: If you are added to a Custom Story, you will be able to see your friends and those that you have not yet added as a friend. You could add every person in that group (if you really wanted to). It's fairly likely that you will get an "add back."
- **Takeovers**: A Takeover is when two Snapchatters swap accounts by sharing their login and password information, and each one logs into the other's account and creates content. The advantage is that you can introduce yourself to a new community of people. Snapchat Takeovers usually last a few hours to an entire day.

  Takeover Tips:
  o  If you are uncomfortable about sharing your password, you can change your current password to a temporary one, and then once the Takeover is completed, you can change it back. You might also want to opt for the two-step verification process as well.
  o  Clearly communicate the guidelines you have about your channel (i.e. swearing, politics, religion etc.). Be savvy about who you collaborate with on any platform. Does the person align with your brand? Do they provide content that resonates with your audience? Is their brand going to go against anything that your brand represents?

o  Be sure you interview your Takeover partner—ask them about what content their audience likes and tailor your content to that, with your flavor, of course.

o  Discuss the time frame for your Takeover, and if your collaboration partner will be allowed to open your messages during that time and respond to them.

o  Provide statistics to your partner: # views, # screenshots, feedback from viewers.

o  Save the Story and be sure to export it to yourself if you are logged into another user's account.

o  Be cognizant of the length of your Story—6 to 20 Snaps max is a good rule of thumb.

o  Let the audience know where they can find you—add your code at the end of your Story and use the Paperclip feature to link out to your other channel(s).

o  Be grateful and thank your Takeover partner.

- **Make Introductions:** Be the connector. Some of my closest friends on Snapchat were introduced to me by a mutual contact. If you have created some close relationships and feel that there are some like-minded individuals who would benefit from connecting with your friends, you can forward someone's Snapcode directly to another user. You may also consider creating a group chat, where multiple people can talk in one threaded conversation. I recommend keeping the group smaller than the maximum allotted if you're not excited about the idea of tons of notifications!

- **Use SnapMap**: I have a suspicion that Snapchat has big plans for SnapMap. While, at this time, you can only see your friends on the map, it may be possible to use this tool to connect with people you don't know in the future. Currently, you can view "hotspots" of activity around your area, indicated by colored spots (like a heat map) indicating areas of higher Snap activity. The colors range from light blue, yellow, orange, to red. Blue indicates lower activity while red means that there might be something going on that you don't want to miss. Checking out the heat-mapped areas could be a great way to decide what to do on a Friday night and you might meet some new Snapfriends.

■　■　■

## Discoverability Hack

Well, here it is. The one and only "hack" I'm including in this book. I'm not a fan of hacks or "gaming the system." I think you have learned by now that I love authenticity. I've got an old school philosophy for a new school medium.

Currently, Snapchat allows users to share their Snaps to "Our Story," which is a collection of Snaps curated by Snapchat.

*Snapchat.com* defines Our Story as:

> *"A place where Snapchatters can build big community narratives together Snaps you submit to Our Story can show up on SnapMap or in Search, grouped together with other Snaps from the same location, event, or about the same topic!*
>
> *Snaps that are submitted to Our Story may be viewable for different amounts of time — some for only a day or two, while others can be seen for much longer[96]."*

Snapchat and many other social platforms are equipped with advanced image recognition software. They can "see" what objects are in your images, identify, and categorize them. They can also do that with audio and text. Snapchat also knows where you are based on your mobile GPS.

If you strategically submit to Our Story, you can improve your discoverability. The key is to include your Snapcode and username on any Snaps that you submit to Our Story so viewers can screenshot and then add you. Without that, people who view your Snaps on a local story won't be able to add you. My assumption is that this will change in the future and we will be able to add people we don't know from local stories easily.

*Note: This method will also work for specific keywords. I included the word "social media" on my Snap submission to Our Story and then I searched for that keyword in the search bar and I did see my own Snap included!

I don't know if this hack will work in the future, but I have personally tried it.

■   ■   ■

## HOW TO GROW AN ENGAGED COMMUNITY

It's one thing to amass friends and followers, but the true measure of any platform shouldn't only be growth. It should be very focused on retention. Engagement should be your primary measurement of success. By creating an engaged audience, you truly create a community of loyal friends. Growing an engaged community is kind of like being a new parent. In the beginning, that little human demands everything all the time and gives nothing in return—be honest, they're not much more than tiny flesh blobs that are either eating, sleeping, or crying. They can't smile at you, and they can't say, "I love you." Yet, regardless of how much energy they require, we still get up at all hours of the night and we consider them the greatest accomplishments of our lives. We have to understand that to grow an authentic community means that we will have to put in the work.

### Snapchat Engagement Tips:

- **Reciprocate**: The law of reciprocity is alive and well on Snapchat—if you watch others, they typically will watch you back. Engagement in Snapchat also means that you will need to spend time watching other people's Stories, even if you may not comment on each one. It comes down to the law of reciprocity—if you want others to watch and support your channel, you'll need to do the same. If you truly, honestly believe that you just don't have time to create consistent content (I'll say you're making excuses), then let your commentary be your content. Meaningful conversations matter—so make time to have them.

- **Be proactive**: The #1 tip I can give to anyone who wants to grow their audience on Snapchat, or any platform, is to proactively engage. What I mean by this is to really LISTEN to what people are talking about—get to know them for a while before you even comment. When you are thoughtful, you're more likely to get a thoughtful response in return. Even better, send them a voice message. You won't always have something clever to say, and sometimes you won't have anything to say at all, but the idea here is that you need to have a strategy that includes committing time to engaging with others. You might even make a personal rule that you don't watch a Story without making at least one comment. You don't have to watch someone's entire Story at once in order to comment.

*Note: If you add an account based on a recommendation from another Snapchatter, let them know who sent you because it immediately establishes a commonality.

- **Promote others**: Sharing the codes of other Snappers that you admire or whom you believe can provide your audience with value is an excellent way to help your community grow. You're not only introducing your audience to another great channel, you're also showing that person some love. If you shout someone out, send them a quick snap alerting them or at least send them the Snap where you shout them out so they know where new followers might be coming from!

- **Connect cross-platform**: Connect with your community on more than one platform. It's a great way for you to learn more about their lives and personal brands, as each social channel has its own language. You might see a more fun side of someone on Snapchat, and then experience their thought leadership content on LinkedIn. For example, someone may see me share marketing tips in a few short Snaps, but then they can watch the entire thirty minute live stream with a much deeper dive on that subject on Facebook.

  Give your audience the option to experience your brand in as many layers as possible, and PLEASE make sure that your brand is cohesive across all social platforms. It ruins the credibility of the brand you are trying to build if one channel is about cars and the other is about flower arrangements. If you're serious about your brand, make sure you are sharing the same message cohesively. This doesn't mean you have to use the exact same content, but I should be able to feel like it's the same brand message from one place to another.

- **Get to know your newest friends**: As new people add you, get to know them right away by tapping on the search bar and then simply scrolling down past the local stories until you see the "New Friends" section—by doing this, you can easily review new friends' Stories without having to sift through your main Story feed.

- **Take the online, offline**: The ultimate way to stay engaged is to meet in person! Often, Snapchatters will organize a meet-up and invite their community to connect in person or at the very least set up an online group video chat through Zoom. us or Skype. As mentioned in my intro, I participated in a meet-up that changed my life and business. Since then, I've connected with many friends "in real life" and hope to continue to do so in the future.

- **Organize your feed**: As your community grows, it can become more challenging to keep up with your must-watch

Snappers. Creating a system that will help you stay engaged and organized so you don't miss out on your favorite channels. While I do believe that eventually Snapchat will offer improved methods of categorization or ways to consume content in a more organized manner, for now you can create your own "emoji" naming system which can help you find the Snappers you want to watch without having to scroll down a feed.

- o Your "username" is set up after downloading the app for the first time. Choose this wisely because you CANNOT change that ever again. The second name is your public Snapchat name, which is how your name will appear to other viewers.
- o Every Snapchatter's public name can be easily edited.
  - Press and hold on Snapchatter's Story or name
  - Tap on the gear icon
  - Select edit name
  - Add the emoji of your choice at the beginning of their name
- o Once you have added an emoji, you can tap the main search bar and enter in that emoji and every Snapchatter's name that begins with that emoji will appear.

*Note: If you are a heavy user of Snapchat and have created a large community, it may become virtually impossible to watch EVERY Story every day. Don't feel guilty, it's OK! Creating an organizational system will help but, you will be less stressed if you accept your limits. Just do what makes you happy or batch your watch time into chunks.

## A note about metrics:

At this time, metrics are limited, but watching your view count will give you an idea if your community is growing, maintaining, or declining. If you find that your view numbers are decreasing, it may mean that you are not as actively creating content, your content may not be resonating with your target audience, or you are not proactively engaging with the community enough.

Personally, I like to measure my engagement by how many comments I may receive on my content—if people are talking to me, then I'm doing something right. Often, what we perceive as killer content may flop, and the stuff we think is just OK hits a home run with the audience.

In the beginning, I urge people not to get wrapped up in numbers. Stay the course, be consistent and after a good amount of time, you can review and track metrics to help you establish a baseline. I know all the marketers reading this right now are clutching their pearls and audibly gasping—yes, I'm not a metrics worshiper—not because I don't believe they aren't important, but because I believe if you are passionate, committed, and keep doing what you're doing, eventually you will earn results.

## Metrics that can be measured:

- # of screenshots
- # of views per Snap in your Story
- Who has viewed each Snap in your Story
- Which of the above viewers you have "added back" as a friend and which ones you have not (if your settings allow anyone to view your Story)

*Note: There are some additional manual metrics you can measure such as Story completion rates and fall-off rate, however this content is merely a basic overview. Additionally, there are third party Snapchat analytics services that (for a fee) will track additional information such as audience insights and competitive benchmarking.*

■  ■  ■

# HOW TO DRIVE TRAFFIC WITH SNAPCHAT

Snapchat now allows users to include links in their Snap content, using the function they call "Paperclip[97]." Now, with one quick swipe up, viewers can access any landing page or website. Those of us using Snapchat to build a professional brand were thrilled when this option became available. Prior to this feature debut, sharing content outside of Snapchat and driving an audience anywhere outside of the app was a terrible user experience.

The goal of any brand should be exposure at scale. The more places your audience sees your brand, the better. When we connect on multiple platforms, our audience can experience our brand in different ways. The content that you share on Snapchat could be very different than the articles on your blog or your live streams on Facebook. Keep in mind, we don't own our content on social sites. We control what happens on our own website or email list, and there's no algorithm in either. Ultimately, any sales or marketing professional will tell you that moving people from your social networks into your database is key for longevity.

## Best practices for using "Paperclip":

- **Share relevant content:** Content in the right context. This is why having a niche is important.
- **Include a call to action:** Tell your audience what to do. It sounds elementary, but it's necessary.
- **Give them a compelling reason to swipe up:** Give your audience some insights on what value they will receive from accessing your link. Give them a sneak peek or top takeaway to catch their interest.
- **Use a trackable link:** Use a Bit. ly or any other custom URL tool which allows you determine the source of traffic.
- **Lead capture:** Email is algorithm free. It's a direct connection to your audience and is permission-based marketing. Using a

landing page with a lead capture component is critical to building your database. Offer a free download or access to webinar in exchange for the visitor's email address.

*Note: If you choose to direct viewers to your Facebook Business Page, you can then create paid advertising campaigns to those who have engaged with your Page or Posts. Also, once people land on your website, as long as you have installed the Facebook Pixel, you can later retarget them with Facebook Ads. It's another way for them to start seeing your brand everywhere.

# 12

## Increase Brand Awareness With Custom Geofilters

*"When you think about the way this aspect of Snapchat's business is structured creates unlimited amounts of inventory. I would not be surprised if in twenty-four months, a stunning amount of the world is covered by these filters. Even now when I go to any public place, I'm seeing at least two or three custom filters in my app. This is a scalable business, and content and context at its finest."*

*- GARY VAYNERCHUK, 2015*

### CREATIVE ADVERTISING

Every minute, Snapchat Geofilters are viewed over 1.5 million times by message or in a Story. That adds up to over 2 billion views per day[98]. A Geofilter is simply a digital "sticker" that is overlaid on top of your Snap that visually enhances its context. Powered by Foursquare and Factual data, Snapchat uses the geolocation of your phone to serve up a variety of daily hyperlocal filters. Some of these filters will be created by Snapchat, while others may be created by paid advertisers, local businesses or everyday Snapchatters. In the early days of Snapchat, only major advertisers were able to create these filters, but now, anyone who has a Snapchat account can easily create a customized Geofilter.

Geofilters can help you grow your brand awareness in a fun and interactive way because they are less invasive that traditional advertisements. They allow the user to engage with the content on their terms. Fun, creative, or well-designed filters can enhance a user's Story. Snapchat will also track metrics such as the number of times your filter was used, and how many times users saw the filter, but swiped past. At this time, they are an affordable and less intrusive form of advertising that can increase your brand reach every time a user shares it with friends in a direct message or to their Story.

Here are three ways to create a Geofilter:

1. (EASIEST) **Create a Geofilter within the Snapchat app**:
   Access pre-designed templates directly within the app itself. This is a quick and easy mobile option that allows you to create and activate a filter on the go.

   - Navigate to "Settings" and scroll down to "On-Demand Geofilters"
   - Select template, location, time, and date (little to no graphic skills required)
   - After you have made your payment, Snapchat will review your Geofilter in, normally, less than 24 hours

2. (EASY) **Access Geofilter templates at *Snapchat.com***:
   Snapchat offers hundreds of pre-designed templates that allow customization, such as color scheme, text overlay, and the ability to upload you and your friends' Bitmoji! If you prefer to work on from your Desktop computer or if you have created your own filter in another design platform, this may be an ideal design method for you.

   - Access *Snapchat.com*
   - Navigate to the "Geofilter" tab
   - Click "Create Your Geofilter"

- Select from Community, Personal or Business options (usually Personal or Business)
- Upload your design or create your design online with a template (minimal design skills required)

3. (LESS EASY) **Design your own Geofilter from scratch using Canva.com** (or any design program):
   This option would be ideal for anyone who wants to create an original design without a template. It will definitely require a little more time and some basic graphic design skills, but it's still very user-friendly.

- Access *Canva.com*
- Click "use custom dimensions"
- Enter 1080 X 1920
- Create your design (some design skills required)
- Download as transparent PNG file
- Follow all the steps in option #2 above

Note: The Canva app for IOS also offers Snapchat Geofilter templates.

■ ■ ■

## TIPS FOR GEOFILTER DESIGN

- **Design**: Don't "over-brand" the design. The best designs are about enhancing the user's Story. If the Geofilter is all about you and your brand, they may not be as excited to use it.
- **Relevant**: Create a design that is relevant to the area or the event to increase usage. For example, if you're creating a Geofilter for a holiday event, make the design match the holiday theme.

- **Location**: When selecting your location, try to target an area where people are likely to take photos or videos: landmarks, sporting events, and popular venues.
- **Formatting**: Be careful not to cover up a lot of the screen with your designs. Geofilters should be an accent or an enhancement not the primary visual. Remember, it's not about you, it's about the user experience.
- **Colors**: Think about the colors of the design—will they stand out, or blend into the background and be hard to see?
- **Text**: Typically, if you are using text, it may be easier for viewers to read if placed on a solid background.
- **Rules**: You cannot use hashtags, URLs, phone numbers, photos of people or @usernames, however, you can use logos. If using a logo or trademark, make sure that you have permission to do so.
- **Timing**: Do not wait until the last minute to create a filter. Your design may not be approved and you'll have to resubmit. Also, the area may already be "sold out" if there are too many filters approved.
- **Awareness**: Consider how to notify users that you have an active Geofilter. You might tell them in person, create on-site signage, or possibly include an announcement in your marketing. I know of some people who have used Facebook Ads to promote their Geofilter contests for specific events as well.
- **Pricing:** Geofilter costs vary based on the length of time or days you want the filter to run, and the size of the area the filter will cover—it could be as little as $6 or up to the thousands. Additionally, if you're thinking about tapping into a huge event like the Olympics, think again—Snapchat already makes advertising deals with big brands during major events, and will either raise prices to extremely high levels, or only offer those geolocation areas to major brands. Snapchat also offers an annual Geofilter option, which means you pay a pre-determined price that auto renews each year (prices may change). Ultimately,

this option could end up saving you money, and offers guaranteed exposure in a specific area long term.

■ ■ ■

## GEOFILTER STRATEGIES

Geofilters are typically a brand awareness, and not a lead conversion, strategy. This means that a Geofilter strategy will not likely lead to an immediate sale. The idea is to increase consumer recall in a subtle way so that when there is a need, they think of you.

Here are some ideas of how your brand can use Geofilters:

- **Take advantage of well attended local events**:
Placing your Geofilter over an area where a lot of potential Snapping may take place is a great way to maximize the eyeballs on your filter.

Dustin Brohm, Owner of *SearchSaltLake.com*, created a custom filter and placed it over the parking lot of the BYU game. The price tag for placing the filter over the actual arena was too expensive, however, Dustin brilliantly decided to place the filter over the parking lot. What do people do in the parking lot of college football games? TAILGATE!!

He spent $70, and 21,157 people saw his Geofilter (467 used it).

Imagine if your brand was over the local arena every game day for an entire season…

- **Create interactive contests at events or conferences:**

  Contests are an excellent way to create engagement with your audience. Create a "Snap to Win" contest where your audience can submit their entries directly to your account with a photo or video Snap of them using your Geofilter. The very best part about receiving a Snap from someone entering a contest is that now you have a way to talk to them. Typically, many people will leave junk email addresses when they register for something via an online form. By using Snapchat, you don't need to capture phone numbers or emails, you simply need to know their username to chat with them.

  Tips for Geofilter contests:

  o Remember to take screenshots of the Snap entries, so you can share that with your community or cross post to other platforms.

  o Consider adding in a creative element that prompts even more personalization and engagement, such as a Geofilter with a "fill in the blank" space for people to write in their own comment.

  o If appropriate for your brand and product, consider sending a coupon or discount code back to every Snap entry (or only the first "x" number of entries).

  o Post your own photo with your Geofilter on your Story and other platforms and tease out clues as to where your conference show booth is, or have your visitors post their own photos with your filter.

  o Host a scavenger hunt with multiple Geofilters around town and require each participant to Snap a photo at each location. You might post clues on your Story and also leverage other platforms to share out clues. This can be a good strategy if you are an established brand and you are launching a new Snapchannel. The contest could require the consumers to add the new channel where they will receive the clues.

- **Host a Geofilter design contest**:
  Get students, clients, or employees collaborating with your brand by hosting a Geofilter design contest where they submit design ideas for a chance to win and have their design selected as the winner. Not only are you getting connected with new people, but you're essentially crowdsourcing the design and getting others involved in the voting. This gives exposure to the designer, your brand, and gets a design made for you! Have them share their participation with their social media channels, and help vote for them to win! You can also advertise your Geofilter contest on other social channels with paid advertising. For example, you could create a Facebook ad promoting the Snapchat contest.

- **Reinforce employee culture:**
  o Create a filter over your office, and engage your employees in taking the best snap of the day.
  o Create a filter for annual company events or team building activities.
  o Use a filter at local career fairs with "we're hiring" or "picture yourself here" theme.
  o Market grand openings for your locations.
    ▪ I love creating a custom Geofilter when meeting with a prospect – it's memorable and a way for you to take a selfie and share it with them and their networks on all platforms. Who else is making them a custom filter on Snapchat? (no one).
  Think of the potential recruiting opportunities when consumers see how much fun their friends are having at your culture-focused company is having every day.

- **Market Pop-up sales**:
  Use a filter during a major public event for nearby business, ex: farmer's market, use a filter that shows your local store with a message like, "today only, Standley's Hand Crafted Candles pop-up shop."

# 13

## Snapchat Advertising

*"Snapchat offers an impressive and growing suite of ad products that tap into three of the 'biggest obsessions consumers have right now': messaging, augmented reality, and visual storytelling."*

- Noah Mallin via *BUSINESSINSIDER.COM*

### SNAP ADS

Snapchat now offers the general public a free ad creation platform to create paid ad campaigns that target specific audiences in a visually engaging format. In May of 2016, Snap, Inc. rolled out their self-serve ad platform for mobile-only, full-screen videos up that are up to 10 seconds in length (access ads dashboard at *Snapchat.com*). These ads appear between users' Stories and also within the premium content in Snapchat's Discover section or Our Story. Data shows that Snap Ads are more effective than other social media ads and that viewers are watching them more than ads on YouTube, Instagram, and Facebook[99].

Snapchat has published the following statistics about Snap Ads[100]:

- Viewed by choice
- Up to 2x higher visual attention vs. comparable platforms

- 2/3 of all Snap Ads play with audio on
- 5x swipe up rate vs. average CTR (click thru rate) on comparable platforms

As a compliment to the online and mobile Snap Ads Manager, Snap Inc. has launched a free online platform to help advertisers easily create Snapchat friendly creative called Snap Publisher[101]. The tool helps convert assets formatted for horizontal viewing easily and offers brands a selection of pre-designed templates. You can find out more about this tool here: *https://snappublisher. snapchat.com.*

As this new offering is still in the early phases, there will surely be many more future developments and product additions.

## Snap Ad types[102]:

All ads will begin with the foundation of a mobile-only vertical video with the option to add an "attachment." Adding an attachment simply means that users can swipe up to access additional information such as a website link, a video, app install, or article.

- **Snap Ad + Article**: Swipe up to access article which can include text or video.
- **Snap Ad + App Install**: Swipe up to access an embedded App Store or Google Play Store page to begin the installation process. Users can install the app in the background while continuing to interact with Snapchat.
- **Snap Ad + Long-Form Video**: Swipe up to watch full-length movie trailers, short films, tutorials, and more.
- **Snap Ad + Web View**: Swipe up to connect directly (within the app itself) to a target website. Users can explore the website, and even complete a purchase, without ever leaving the Snapchat app.

## Snap Ad metrics[103]:

Snapchat will provide advertisers with the following measurements (not a complete list):

- **Viewability**: How much attention ads receive (time spent viewing etc.)
- **Reach**: How many people saw the ad, and the age, gender and other demographic info of viewers
- **Resonance**: Analysis of brand awareness, brand opinion and favorability
- **Reaction**: Determine offline lift in sales resulting from ad
- **Verification**: How many times ad was served

Some additional measurements are available based upon the specific ad format.

## Snap Ads audience targeting[104]:

Like Facebook Ads, Snap Ads offer targeting, based on user behaviors and demographics (over 300 audience categories). Additionally, Snap Ads will allow advertisers to match emails, create Lookalike audiences, and connect with people who have engaged with your Snap Ads, Geofilters, or Lenses in past campaigns. Lastly, Snapchat works with third party partners like Oracle and PlaceIQ that can tap into offline purchase behaviors, movie viewership, and even locations that Snapchatters have visited throughout their day!

Examples of interest based targeting options (not a complete list):

- **Lifestyles/Hobbies:** Beauty, Fashion, Investing, Streaming Video, Hip Trends, Fast Food Junkies
- **Music:** Country, Indie, Festivals
- **Activities/Sports:** Snow Sports, Running, College Football
- **News/Entertainment:** Film, TV, Comedy, Celebrity News, Political News

# 14

## Social Selling With Snapchat

*"Thought leadership happens when you're willing to have your brand stand for more than what you sell."*

- SETH PRICE, AUTHOR AND SPEAKER

Let's face it, operating a for-profit business requires that, at some point, you begin to make money. We need to sell our products and services in order to make a profit, and using social networks to generate business is critical in a modern day marketplace. Social platforms can be incredible conduits to connect with potential customers, and a platform that positions your brand as an expert resource. Unfortunately, what typically happens is people forget their manners when they're behind a keyboard or a screen. They become pushy and bold, asking for the sale before they even build rapport because it's so easy to send a bunch of direct messages to their social sphere. They tell themselves, "well, eventually someone will say yes, either because they feel guilty, or because they are actually interested." We listen to hardcore sales gurus who extol the benefits of asking for what you want and their warnings that if you don't ask, you don't get. Perhaps the worst tactic is the let's-send-some-messages-and-then-I-hit-you-with-a-sales-pitch that comes out of nowhere. This is where social selling comes into play.

A *salesforce.com* report[105] defines social selling as:

> *"A lead-generation technique grounded in social media. It allows salespeople to directly interact with their prospects on various social media platforms. By challenging the norm of how sales "happens", salespeople, customer service agents, and even marketers can now reach out to customers through their preferred social platforms. The success behind social selling rests in the bedrock of the community network and the trust that is built off the back of it."*

Social selling is about developing relationships through social networks and messaging platforms as part of the sales process. It's driven by creating or curating contextual and value-based content, and giving, helping, and then giving some more. It attracts potential clients to you organically because it's rooted in generosity. It requires a brand to listen to consumers' needs and then share relevant content that will answer their questions and solve their problems. The end goal of providing so much value you're your brand earns consumer trust, which leads them to want to do business with you.

Generosity is a skill that they don't teach you in marketing or sales courses. What happened to the old days of earning someone's business, not simply trying to buy it or intimidate them into a forced, "yes, I'll try your product," attack by direct message?

Two of my favorite Seths sat down for a chat about a "return on trust." Seth Price, marketing and branding speaker and author, interviewed Seth Godin about what it takes to be a "generous marketer." Godin shares the reason why trust is the most important factor in any businesses success:

> *"Even if your goal is make a lot of money, the best way to make a lot of money is to be more trusted…Whether you are a banker, a lawyer or*

*a dog-walker, the most-trusted person is able to charge a premium. The most-trusted person will grow faster, the most-trusted person will find more people willing to go with them on a journey.*

*This return on trust is overlooked by people who are playing a different game.*

*If you're a card hustler, then you only want to be trusted for an hour until you leave town. My point about the internet is that you can't leave town.[106]* "

*- SETH GODIN*

Mic drop.

The only thing that you have to sell is yourself—it is irrelevant what kind of product or service you may be selling, what matters is that your audience be sold on YOU. Don't be afraid that you're giving away too much information—if people really want to learn how to do something, they can Google their faces off to find out how. With so many people hocking their wares on the social media street corner, today's consumer really appreciates someone who will give away their knowledge without expectation. I'm not saying you shouldn't make money off of your experience—of course you should! What I'm saying is that in order to reach the point where you can monetize, you're going to have put in a lot of hours without a payday.

*I highly recommend reading the book authored by Seth Price and Barry Feldman called: The Road to Recognition: The A-to-Z Guide to Personal Branding for Accelerating Your Professional Success in The Age of Digital Media*

If you're planning on using Snapchat for selling, here are some important tips:

- **Be generous:** I find that the most successful brands give away their best stuff. They don't hide the goods behind a paywall. They share and then share some more. If you think you can outsmart Google, think again. If people really want to know something and they have enough time and determination, they can find out anything. You could easily offer your community FREE fifteen minute sessions where they can ask you anything or you can provide them with a mini business consultation and offer tips with no expectation. (You can call them right through Snapchat—how convenient). You might send your products to your community free of charge and let them know WHY you felt they would benefit from using the product. Never ever pitch your services during these consultations. Karma is the ultimate loyalty program, and what goes around comes around.
- **Personalize it:** Instead of making a public Story about wanting to offer free coaching sessions, send a personalized direct message (preferably video) to your friend, and list why you want to offer your expertise (i.e. you love their energy or their authenticity or passion, and you have some ideas that could really amp up their success).
- **Prove it:** Prove to people that you are an expert through your content. They will see what you do and then you don't have to "sell" them.
- **Send them good stuff:** Send valuable content that a specific person will appreciate—I call this Newspaper Clipping Mentality because my parents clip out articles or comics that reminds them of me, or pertains to something I am interested in. It shows the recipient that you are LISTENING, not just hearing what they say.

- **Interview them:** Livestream, podcast or a good ol' fashioned blog article are great ways to highlight your community AND help you create great content.
- **Ask them:** There is one question that is possibly the most important one you can ask, "how can I help you today?"

If you want to generate leads or create meaningful relationships, the formula is the same: help people by providing them with information that matters to them or will improve their lives without obligation.

Just do the right thing.

# 15

## The Medium Is The Message

Professor Marshall McLuhan studied how mass media affected human behavior. He coined several oft used phrases such as "age of information" and "global village," and even predicted the Internet 35 years prior to its launch[107].

(He was even honored with his very own Google Doodle, so you know he was kind of a big deal.)

He believed that because of media, society was converging into one collective ecosystem, one organism. His most famous phrase was that "the medium is the message," meaning, it's not the tool or the platform that matters, it's what we learn from using it.

This book is about Snapchat but it's more importantly, about what it taught us about communication through a camera, and how we find communities today. It made it normal for us to express ourselves using our own personal media, our photos and videos—which aren't just for preserving memories anymore.

A lot of people say that Snapchat's dying, that everyone is moving to Instagram Stories, and a year from now, Snapchat may not exist, but that doesn't matter. It has already changed our behaviors and expectations.

To be very honest, Snapchat is harder than other platforms because you can't buy likes and you can't outsource being you.

That's why it's human.

Apply these suggestions and best practices to any visual social platform, and it can help you build a powerful personal brand.

Remember, authenticity beats an algorithm every time.

# Part 4
## Allow Me To Introduce ...

The people whom I have included within this section are only a small portion of the amazing community that I have connected with through Snapchat. There are many, many more incredible creators that I engage with on a daily basis and selecting only a limited number of accounts to highlight was a challenge. I specifically selected the following accounts because the creators are using Snapchat to develop their personal brands, educate, entertain, raise awareness or create a community.

## Business:

- Helen Blunden @**activatelearn**: Helen lives in Australia and is a Workplace Learning Practitioner. She helps people activate the way they learn, connect and collaborate with each other when their workplace is under constant change and transformation. Besides having a super cool accent, Helen loves knitting, books and all things tech.

   *"Snapchat allows me to capture the mood and the moments of the day through space and place to create a storyline of my life and my projects. It allows people to build a portfolio of their work - their own mini movie of their life - that can support their professional and personal goals. It's connected me with microbiologists, marketers, doctors, academics, teachers, real estate agents, engineers from different parts of the world who I would never have come into contact with and who have broadened my view and perspective."*

- David Holzmer, PhD @**davidholzmer:** David is a consultant and researcher investigating how organizations construct the experience of change and what that now means for us in an era of accelerating communication and nearly continuous upheaval. He has documented his journey to becoming a PhD via Snap, writes for *leadx.org* and also loves walking along the beaches of Cape May and eating tacos on a regular basis.

*"Snapchat is amazing! It offers a level of engagement and immediacy that is not possible on the other popular platforms. For me the key is the disappearing content. Some people see that as a downside, but not me. Just like in real-life, on Snapchat you're not valued for simply a catchy tagline or a well-posed shot; you're valued for the sincerity of your interactions day and day out. Unlike the other popular platforms, that's allowed me to a tight network of like-minded others that has consistency and depth. In my book, that makes Snapchat the most authentically "social" of all the social media outlets!"*

- Sabba Quidwai **@askmsq**: Sabba is an Apple Distinguished Educator, design thinking advocate and keynote speaker who served as the Director of Innovative Learning at the Kleck School of Medicine of USC. Her mission: to help empower people to become creative problem solvers. Sabba also shares her love of travel and fashion for women in the workplace.

*"When you begin with empathy, what you think is challenged by what you learn. Snapchat provides us with a medium to share our stories, spark conversations and create a world that is technology driven and human centered."*

- JoAnn Krall **@joannkrall**: JoAnn is a professional organizer who supports and guides entrepreneurs. She helps them get organized in their home, business, and life so they can be more productive, peaceful and prosperous. JoAnn shares her expertise through Snapchat and has created several hilariously funny "signature" characters by strategically using the ever-changing face Lenses.

*"I have built an incredible number of both professional and personal relationships. More quickly than any other platform to date. I think of snapchat as the hub of my social media strategy. Creating relationships there and then connecting across other platforms has increased my reach and credibility."*

- Kim Gaskill **@ecotek**: Kim is a curious traveler who is often driving cross-country to explore the world and share it via Snapchat. She is an entrepreneur who helps small businesses leverage digital media and marketing to build their brand. When she's not on her front porch, you can find Kim volunteering in a different state every month!

*"When I explored the possibilities in Snapchat I had no idea what an impact it would have on how I communicate with the world. Snapchat has become my number one go to app for connecting with my friends across the globe, sharing and supporting others and exploring the possibilities inside the creative side of my brain. Through Snapchat I am able to tap into my inner 'goofball' and not afraid to let people see it! Snapchat has not only changed how I share my story but with whom I share it. My Snapchat community makes me a better person. I laugh more. I create more. I share more. I connect more."*

- Leslie Gustafson LMFT, CST **@ldgustafson:** As a licensed therapist and a television sex, marriage and relationship expert, Leslie shares her unique expertise with the Snapchat community. Her central mission in life is to inspire men and women, through education and psychotherapy, to know themselves, live authentically and passionately, enhance their relationships, and build lives centered on truth and wisdom. Leslie loves wine, food and music you can groove to! When she's not on television, you can find her outdoors or working on her next piece of art!

*"In over 500 days of live streaming myself, my business and nearly my whole life on Snapchat, my life and business have been amazingly and positively impacted more than any other Social Media Platform to date. I'm a Therapist, Coach, Author, TV Personality, Radio Personality, Wife, Mom, Grandma, Adventurer and Artist. Snapchat has benefitted each one of these roles. I have gained personal empowerment, increased confidence in speaking and entertaining, comfort in being vulnerable in a broader audience, sharpened my skill of presenting well on camera, as I've allowed my whole personality to be seen and heard. Snapchat has given me the opportunity to display my creativity, my voice, my dancing ability, my love for food, wine and travel, my intellectual acumen, my heart and my full personality – an Introvert who acts like an Extrovert. And perhaps most importantly, I have developed friendships and deep personal relationships that I will treasure all my life.*

*Businesswise, Snap has helped me expand my social media community to 20,000 strong, build significant business relationships and educate and inspire in my areas of expertise- sex, relationships, psychology, mental health, family life and lifestyle issues. In addition, I have answered hundreds of confidential questions via my "Ask The Therapist Show," launched our first "Big Love" Online Marriage class which was marketed and populated primarily through Snapchat, gathered past and current therapy and coaching clients who have come to "know, like and trust" me (particularly important in my line of work), sell our book Amazing Intimacy, strengthen our private Facebook Support Community and migrate friends/followers to my other social media platforms. Every day, it provides me with a path to strategically market my business without feeling like I'm at marketing at all. How cool is that!*

*I can do whatever I want on Snap spontaneously at any time, and I do. I have a consistent viewership that I have the privilege of connecting with every day in a highly personal, face to face modality. In this I aim to develop authentic relationships and give over what I know to help them grow and create amazing lives while contributing to the nearly communal snap community that is unique to Snapchat. Snapchat is highly creative, intimate, and easy to use once understood and I have had a blast being there which is critical to me to sustain longevity in doing anything."*

- John Kapos **@chocjohnny:** Known around the world as "Chocolate Johnny," John is a professional chocolatier and small business owner living in Australia who takes his followers behind the scenes using Snapchat. He shares the magic of his sweet life through social and as an international speaker, teaches brick and mortar stores how to use social platforms to reach new customers. It's rumored that John may even employ his very own chocolate making Oompa Loompas at his store, Perfection Chocolates.

*"I didn't see the potential of Snapchat for my business until I was Snapping my customers and they started to respond back. The main problem is that businesses still think Snapchat is for kids. It's a market already waiting for these small businesses to utilize Snapchat. The problem is that they can't see a return on investment immediately. If they let go of their fear of Snapchat and social media they can use it and get their customers and staff involved more involved. Go have fun, be creative and remember, you can't make mistakes. It's all about being raw and real. Don't forget the community who are watching you. Without your community, you have zero." (Excerpt from interview on customfilterz.com)*

- Haida Baig **@heidiapi6**: A 26 year old, born and bred Londoner, content creator, author, web designer and fitness fanatic, Haida shares her love for connecting with people via Snapchat. Haida shares positivity and her reflections on creating community through a variety of social platforms. She is also documenting her own book writing process and adores all things sports!

*"Snapchat is always engaging and keeps changing the game; but for me its true beauty lies in how it breaks down the barriers of communication, how it helps in developing the confidence to create and how it builds an interesting and connected community."*

- Jeff Standley **@jeff.standley**: Jeff and his daughter Mallori created their own business and document the process of a homegrown start-up (read: in their kitchen) through Snapchat. This DIY team makes handcrafted candles, bath bombs, body butters and lip balms. Jeff loves to work out at the crack of dawn in bright pink shoes and spends the rest of his time working on the never-ending backyard improvements.

*"The thing I love most about Snapchat is the community and the audience you build. You know for certain that it's authentic and earned. It's work to get that audience, work to maintain it and the interactions are true. You can't fake it."*

- Eric Triplett **@theponddigger:** Eric is a Waterscape Design & Construction Specialist and is obsessed with building ponds! A super niche channel, Eric can teach viewers a thing or two about what it takes to build a brand. He documents the adventures, challenges and wins he and his team experience on a daily basis. The passion that Eric has for his career let alone for life itself, is inspiring. Follow him along as he Snaps his day and shares some pond pro tips along the way!

*"Snapchat changed the game for me on social media. From sharing my content creation for business to communicating with my kids about what's*

*for dinner, Snapchat hands down my all-time favorite tool. I simply don't leave home without it!"*

- Jessica Smith **@jessnesssnaps** (yes, three "s"): Jessica is a Career Coach and podcast host of *Career Coaching with Jessness*. She's a self-love author, finishing her first book titled, *'YOUR TWENTIES'* set to release later this year. Jess' coaching philosophy centers around removing the external noise and reflecting inward to discover our inner wisdom, or in her words, finding our 'ness. When we tune into our 'ness, we effortlessly flow with life, have more confidence, and invite joy into every day.

*"As a career coach, I'm passionate about helping people express less about what they do and more about who they are as a person. Snapchat IS that concept in an app form. It gives people, businesses and brands the opportunity to connect with the human behind the highlight reel you only see on your newsfeed."*

- Danica Wooley **@dailydanica**: Danica is a recovering legal professional turned stay-at-home-entrepreneur, NHL hockey wife and mom who is building her own personal business through Snapchat. Danica shares her insights on how to use social platforms to sell the right way. Her daily adventures include her puppy Daley, her life as a #boymom and her interesting neighbors.

*"Snapchat was something special that I approached with little expectation. I immediately found that there was something different about the way storytelling felt empowering and it changed forever the way I viewed the future of social. The face to face interaction, the exchange of ideas, the supportive community I became a part of made me realize that my network of friendship and partnership was truly global. My life has been enriched by this medium, very unexpectedly."*

## Storytellers:

- Bill Flannery **@texasbrush1**: Bill sells plates which is probably the most unsexy thing you can sell. He uses Snapchat to educate salespeople on how to best use a camera first strategy and a little humor to sell any product, no matter how exciting it may or may not be. He is the proud owner of a patented product called The Texas Grill Brush and the creator of a one-of-a-kind Snapchat group story before that even existed. He invented the "Soup Bowl Challenge" and tasked 16 people from around the globe to create an original short film using Snapchat about this bowl. It was quirky, original and fun but the real brilliance behind it was that people he had never even met were "selling" his products for him. He's the only Snapchatter who is worth watching that still doesn't look at the camera.

  *"It's the best platform to meet new people. It's more of a natural way to communicate and grammar, editing does not apply so you get to see the real person not some polished up edited version. I've expanded my network, some of which I've formed working relationships with [while] others are just friends that I might reach out to for advice or vice versa. The intimacy of relationships happens super-fast on Snapchat."*

- Chris Baier **@baierman11**: An award-winning Writer, Creative Director and Blogger. Chris' advertising campaigns have been honored at Cannes Lions and the One Show. He has featured in Adweek, Communication Arts and Lurzer's Archive. Most recently, he co-produced his first film *Unstuck: An OCD Kids Movie* and documented the process with Snapchat. Chris' own daughter was the inspiration for the film. When not working, he's creating inspirationless quotes and wondering what subway ads are all about.

*"Other platforms let you connect, follow and find new people, which is fine. The chat + story aspect of Snapchat lets you get to know people in a way that is 1000x more personal. Also, Snap was the first platform that I never felt guilty about unfollowing people. The first platform where I realized numbers didn't matter or reflected your status. It's my favorite TV channel and so I only want to watch the shows/people I enjoy. I encourage others to do the same.*

*When big moments came about in our [film] production, my SC community was always there, unprompted, to promote, shoutout and lend a kind word. They also became my army on other platforms, amplifying our message and outreach especially on Twitter."*

- Cammy Murray **@cammysutra6**: A Content Creator by trade, Cammy is perhaps one of the most talented and entertaining storytellers who uses Snapchat as a medium to create cinematic "Snapfilms." His has a clear passion for documenting and creating beautiful, cohesive stories with Snapchat and some editing skills. He's got a wicked accent and a deep love of all things Celine Dion.

*"Pre-Snapchat, social media had slumped into a state of hyper-normalization; a digital world of algorithms, metrics, newsfeeds, and sponsored posts. When Snapchat arrived on the scene, which both promoted and celebrated putting people first, it provided a platform focused on innovation, creativity and authentic storytelling, effectively creating a new 'social language', taking the selfie from an expression of vanity, to that of a means of communication.*

*Snapchat changed the game."*

- Nick Rishwain **@njrish**: Nick is a VP of Client Relations for a legaltech company and a frequent live video show host on topics that range from social media to tech (LegalTech Live and Social Chatter). Nick has a deep desire to improve access to justice and lower the cost of legal services through the use of technology and collaboration. Nick's sense of humor is contagious as he offers black and white Snap content intended to be satirical in nature. His ride or die co-pilot, a senior-aged Chihuahua named Tica, manages to tolerate his antics.

*"Snapchat gives me the freedom to have more fun in content creation, without having to explain the content. Also, it is nice to communicate with people through short video clips. It is nice to see their face and watch their mannerisms. Helps me to better know the person with whom I'm communicating."*

- Joe Wilson **@joewilsontv**: Joe is a producer of several live-action and graphic novel series, a former standup comic and live video host using Snapchat to tell stories. He coined the phrase "we are all famous to a few people" and is the creator of the #frozensnapfriday movement. Frozen snapping was inspired by the 1980's show *Police Squad* where actors simply stood motionless while the credits rolled. Hundreds of people all over the world participate in these 10-second, no-blink Snaps. He drinks more coffee than any human I know and loves his wife, KZ and his gray cat, Mike.

*"I love Snapchat because it can't be automated and the communication/ engagement is always with one person at a time. It's also the one-to-one engagement that cannot be faked because you're always talking to one person at a time. I [also] like the variety of possibilities, even with just the basics of sound and camera. Snapchat can be radio if you put your finger over the Lens. It can be a slide show, a comedy sketch stage, a place to tell stories of all kinds. Add in filters, Lenses and some of the other developments that have appeared recently and you can make Snapchat whatever you want it to be and have fun doing so. I am definitely having*

*more fun on SC than other platforms. Because the content is temporary, only available for 24 hours and can be tapped through if it's boring, I feel like it's the best place to try stuff that wouldn't fly on other platforms."*

- Angela Hursh **@webmastergirl**: Angela is a Content Team Leader in the Marketing Department of the Cincinnati Public Library. A self-described girl from rural northern Ohio who loved libraries so much that she grew up to promote them. She worked for more than 20 years as a broadcast TV journalist before leaping to library marketing. She manages to make working in a library seem like one of the most interesting jobs in the world! Angela has access to an incredible variety of historic books which she features daily on her "Bonkers Books" show.

*"Snapchat has changed my professional life by helping me to show the inner workings of a library and bounce ideas off various and diverse groups of people. It's also connected me to groups that I would never have met! I did a presentation at a library conference last year on marketing to teens and I used Snapchat to survey my daughter's friends and run various points past them to get their feedback."*

- Aaron Adel **@bizaaron**: Aaron is a Social Media Consultant who managed the social media and website for a major Canadian consumer products brand for 4 years before deciding it was time to stop managing other people's social media and start teaching them to do it themselves. Each day he converses with his network through private chat and tells stories of little to no personal consequence, yet somehow people are drawn to his "stories about nothing" perhaps due to Snapchat's incredible ability to convey his personality.

*"The beauty of Snapchat's ecosystem is that there is never anything there that allows you to discriminate before taking any action. Snapchat allows people to express the true essence of themselves through video in a raw*

*unedited format. While other social networks offer more polished and refined versions of content, this can be limiting when it comes to getting to know who people really are. I remember when Instagram first came out with stories and a few of the people who I had only known through photographs for years began posting videos of themselves and I realized that I didn't even know the person I had been connected with that whole time in their truest form. It was quite shocking actually, because I had completely different ideas of what they might have been like in person.*

*Snapchat is like having a Toastmasters club in your pocket. If you show up and record yourself on video every single day for two years (or even for one month), and you make sure you connect with a network that includes people who are smarter than you in some areas and can give you constructive feedback, you will see a marked improvement in your presentation, communication and storytelling skills, I guarantee it. This in turn will improve your ability lead, coach and even mentor others if that's what you want to do. Many people obtain clearer realizations of their passions after Snapchat; I've seen this happen to many people and it's pretty incredible.*

*Now that Facebook and its family of social networks have copied Snapchat's Story feature, many people are led to believe that this was the most important part of Snapchat. This couldn't be further from the truth. You must plan to give the private chat aspect of Snapchat priority if you want to build your network. Stories are supplementary to this; it's simply the icing on the cake. While more people are posting and watching Instagram Stories than on Snapchat, Snapchat's most important feature to their main users is the private chat and the user experience is much preferred over Instagram, Messenger and Facebook Direct."*

- Chris Strub **@chrisstrub**: The first man to live stream in all 50 states. Chris is a Millennial Keynote Speaker and author of the book *50 States, 100 Days* which chronicles his once-in-a-lifetime cross country trip volunteering with youth organizations (which he documented using Snapchat). Chris has a prolific background in social media management and a heart for service. Keep an eye out in your state for his "Honda Hotel" during his next road trip!

*"You are the sum of the five people you spend the most time with. What Snapchat gives everyone is direct access to some of the brightest, most creative and supportive people on the planet. By providing a window into the personal and professional lives of these thought leaders, as well as a channel to communicate with them directly, Snapchat has advanced the art of international relationship building to almost unimaginable levels. Now other social media channel has allowed me to build and cultivate such a diverse, encouraging and action-oriented network, with previously unthinkable face-to-face interactions (even if those faces don flower crowns or bunny ears) becoming commonplace."*

- Tina Robinette **@tinafightsfire:** Tina is a mom, a wife and a Fire Marshall! She's passionate about serving and protecting her community and may just be Wonder Woman in disguise. Join her daily life protecting and serving and for her weekly installment of "#TakeTwoTuesday" where she showcases her Snapfams' hilarious #onetakesnaps and bloopers!

*"Snapchat has been a way for me to express myself without feeling as though I need to censor my personality. I utilize Snapchat purely for personal use, but it has allowed me to meet many people across the world! It allows me to share my life adventures and create friendships in a positive, uplifting way!"*

- Michelle Brown **@q_brownie**: Michelle is a mom, wife and teacher who loves music, dancing and singing. She's passionate about social media and sharing positivity with her community, usually, through a lip-sync battle or maybe even a living room dance off!

*"The friendships I've made are what I love the most about Snapchat. I found that I have so much in common with so many people that are not physically in my life, and yet have made a big impact on me through Snapchat. I have met teachers, housewives, professionals, comedians and so many other interesting people that have touched my life. I truly would be missing so much if I weren't on Snapchat. It's amazing how you can care so much, laugh so much, and learn so much from people you have never met in person from all around the world."*

- Ben Traviss **@thisisabsorb:** Ben is a talented musician who has been writing and producing rap music for over a decade. His stage name is ABSORB and he shares his journey behind the scenes of how he creates his lyrics, recording tracks and his performance prep. He's a live streamer and creator of his signature hashtag #PTFAD- you'll have to add him on Snap to find out what it means!

*"I love Snapchat because there is no other platform around today which makes you feel as close to the journey of those you're connected with. Using this micro vlog technology, we have the ability to capture, create and share our stories with the world; whether it be documenting a hectic twenty-four hours or a journey that lasts for several months, maybe even years. There are people who I've connected this using this amazing platform who I now consider to be my friends rather than merely online acquaintances which shows you how powerful this platform can be. There's nothing quite like it and it's now an integral part of how I market my brand."*

- Vanessa Workman **@theislandrum** (one "d"): Vanessa is the Founder and Executive Editor of travel and lifestyle blog, *theislanddrum.com*. She began her career in Florida in the medical field, but her first love was travel. Her passion for the exotic brought her to Malaysia where she shares the local lifestyle through Snapchat. When she's not writing, Vanessa can be found hanging out with her chickens, Brendan and Grace.

*"Snapchat scared me at first, because I thought the entire world would be able to witness my learning curve, baby steps. I was rewarded with my brave plunge with the immediate awareness that there are indeed privacy settings as well as 'viewers' to actually gather. And by gathering I don't mean spamming other feeds or buying 'followers'. Suddenly a whole world of real communication appeared. Real people from all walks of life were suddenly at my doorstep and I at theirs. A breath of fresh air to suddenly engage with other humans instead of the constant 'influencers' and marketing gurus (of other social media channels). But the magic of Snapchat is that users can be human as well as marketing gurus at the same time; the quiet family of three Snapping their vacation 'for fun' are also influencing. The unassuming carpenter Snapping his daily lunch options becomes an influencer. The audience and reach is diverse and the potential for whatever the 'cause' is great. I have learned through Snapchat connections to accept my own visual as well as vocal short comings and embraced this social media not only as a marketing tool but as an amazing way to simply meet new friends."*

- Karen Geraghty **@blissbakery:** Karen's channel is filled with incredible travel, storytelling and food! She is the creator of the *yankeedoodlepaddy.com* blog that highlights her life as an American-turned-Londoner who's passionate about food and all things Irish. Her Snapchannel will make you want to book the next flight to anywhere she's traveling! Don't miss her #TelltheTruthThursday and #FoodieFieldTripFriday Snaps!

*"I LOVE Snapchat. For someone who isn't very tech savvy, every day on Snapchat is a miracle. I am a chef, so I'm more of a pots and pans person. Another caveat is that I didn't start my social media career until*

*I was 50 years old. Snapchat saved my life. Okay, that may sound dramatic, but it is true. Moving from my soul home Ireland to the U.K. in 2015 wasn't part of my life plan. I missed the Emerald Isle something terrible. But staying connected through Snapchat helped me feel a part of the culture I longed for. I was able to thrive on Snapchat through producing content and regular segments. Some said I had implemented an editorial calendar, but the truth is that it was only out of necessity to create a commUNITY. More than two years later I have met many of my Snapfam in person and am proud to call them friends. I have been so grateful to Snapchat for designing an app that allows for fun, creativity, bonding, support and also provides users a platform to fulfill their purpose in life!"*

## Positivity:

- Janelle Romero **@thesassysurvivr** (no "o"): Janelle is a cancer survivor and vlogger dedicated to show, share, and support her community with a lifestyle of simple soul-utions for success. Janelle shares daily tips on how to change your life one day at a time with a positive attitude. Her daily dose of silliness coupled with her big-hearted spirit are guaranteed to make you smile.

   *"Snapchat has always been a space to really just be the most real version of myself. I am able to show my goofiness, and hopefully make people laugh while sharing motivation. The platform has become my favorite to use since users are able to see a fast insight into someone's life, and easily strike up a conversation from there. Because of the desire to continue the conversation from a stranger's Snap, I have made incredible friendships."*

- Sandra Centorino **@sayitforward**: The ultimate Positive Disruptor, Sandra is on a mission to create Social Good. Her movement is #SayitForward in which she creates products that encourage others to become inspired and then pay it forward.

A self-proclaimed Positivity Practitioner, Sandra is an international educator and speaker. Sandra's Facebook Live show hosts a wide variety of inspirational speakers and professional marketers and guest appearances by her favorite emoji.

*"Snapchat was the beginning of me growing a community - you never know how or when you might touch another life."*

- Bree Palmer **@breepalm**: An advocate for Mental Health Initiatives, Bree is passionate about raising awareness and erasing stigmas. With a passion for social media and connecting the world with people that make a difference, she is the creator of *The Amazing Human Series*, a blog and live streaming show featuring people who are not only inspirational, but also relatable.

*"I love Snapchat because it has lead me to discover so many Amazing Humans from all over the world!"*

- Lauri Rottmayer **@laurirottmayer**: Lauri is a former pageant queen turned social media lover and author of two books *Pageant Savvy* and *Social Media for the Savvy Pageant Girl*. She loves to throw around some heavy weights at the gym and serves as the Functional Aging Specialist at Athletic Mission Performance Center. She and her hubby are world travelers and love a good road trip. When not at the gym, Lauri spends time with her Glambaby and new puppy.

*"I love offering Snapchat to my clients as part of their social media strategy. It gives such behind the scenes look at a brand that could be incredible if done right. On a personal level, Snapchat is my favorite social platform. I have developed the closest friendships through the magic of Snapchat. My goal on any social network is to be able to have coffee with a friend anywhere in the world. The relationships I've made here*

*are more complete than any I've made elsewhere. I love the creativity and crafting my story every day."*

- Salina Walker **@iamlovesvoice**: Salina is the founder of A Glimpse of Encouragement, a movement focused on inspiring hope so that others will look forward to the greatness that the future holds. A faith-centered mother and wife, Salina shares her uplifting words and #FaithFriday with her community. Her channel is filled with uplifting thoughts and also her hilarious mom moments!

*"I love Snapchat because it's an outlet for people to share their thoughts and feelings more intimately than on any other platform. This allows me to connect with people and reach out to those that need 'a glimpse of encouragement.' My mantra is: love others to LIFE."*

- Amber Nore **@ambercamille76**: Amber is an avid reader & American goofball who uses her Snapchat story to promote the Arts. She loves to create stories with other social media enthusiasts. When not Snapping, she can be found dancing or with her nose in a book. Amber is a proud single mama who works as a district leader in the retail industry. She is currently developing two one-act plays for production. Don't miss her #TeaandTomes book review Snapshow!

*"I love Snapchat because it provides me a deeply connected community space to share my passions, joys, goofball ideas, frustrations and to document my daily life. In addition, I have been able to meet, connect and collaborate with people from around the world. I have gained friendships, created collaborative stories and learned new things (from cooking to business, money tips, new music and more). I am blessed that my participation with the Snapchat social media platform has led to positive tangible differences in my life.*

- Adam Purcell **@purcelliraptor**: "Service through social" is at the heart of Adam's channel. He's the founder of #CaringCounts which is a movement focused on creating personal, emotional, memorable and shareable customer experiences. Adam speaks on topics such as creating employee culture, customer experience and using social media to spread ideas that catch on. Warning: Cute Kids alert when watching his channel!

*"The beautiful thing about Snapchat is that the conversation is the content. If you're not a big influencer or recognized name, you don't have to worry because in Snapchat, simply talking and engaging with people is considered great content here. There's no other platform that can help you build deep relationships than Snapchat."*

- Katie Miller @**katiesmiller**: It may not be possible to meet someone more selfless than Katie. She devotes her time serving the tangible and spiritual needs of struggling families in Southeast Michigan. She's an accomplished baker who has been known to mail her Snapchat family "sweets from the homefront" which is also the name of her website. Her mission is to lead with love and ensure that no one in her community ever goes hungry. She loves ballet and spending time with her fur babies.

*"I love Snapchat because it opens the door to a candid behind the scenes world. Real connections and friendships are built through interaction. Honestly, the raw sharing of hopes, dreams, and things that stir the heart to action and sometimes trials is compelling. People share resources, ideas, teach and encourage. That's just at the surface – there is so much more."*

## Health and Nutrition:

- Natx Wang @**natxwang:** Natx is a certified nutritionist who started her own Snapchat health movement called #SweatSnap where people all over the world share their fitness snaps to help themselves and others stay accountable and inspired. Natx shares nutrition and health tips in between her world travels and her in-home workouts with her four-legged side-kick, Cupid.

*"I was lurking on Snapchat and wasn't sure what I was supposed to post on it… It was until one day I decided to publicly commit to the 8 or 10 people who were watching my stories that I was going to start a workout program. I started posting my post workout selfies, also known as #SweatSnap to the squad. From there, it just grew. People who wanted accountability for their workouts started sending me their #SweatSnaps as well. It gave me permission to follow my passion, and an audience that I can reach out to, and help. I love seeing all the 'before and afters' and witnessing the changes in my friends in their own journey. Snapchat made it possible because of how easy it is to interact. I love watching my friends' stories because I can celebrate their wins and understand their struggles through their lens. I love it when I give them advice to try and they start posting it on their story. I get to see how they adapt to it and give tips to encourage them to keep going."*

- Dallas Peck **@dalpisme**: Dallas is a personal trainer, entrepreneur and daddy of one creating a fitness business from the ground up. Always there to offer a workout tip or just a word of encouragement, he uses Snapchat to share his journey as a new business owner and giving viewers a peek into the startup lifestyle.

*"Snapchat is so organic and I would have never thought I would actually meet people from an app. I see these people every day on my timeline and think of them as family! There isn't another app that has figured out this type of engagement!"*

- Sara Boykan MC, LPC **@itsboink**: Sara is a licensed professional counselor and Periscope influencer who has taken her passion for fitness to the next level sharing health and fitness tips through Snapchat. Recently, she's documented her first pregnancy with Snapchat and launched Project Potential which includes her personal program for fit pregnancies!

*"Snapchat turns a cold market into a warm one faster than you can boil water for your mac & cheese! Behaviorism favors others' ability to see your mannerisms, hear your inflection, and share your personality in a way that is warm and organic."*

- Gina Hansen @healthyhulagirl: Gina is a part-Hawaiian island girl who loves outdoor fun, travel, dancing and social media. She is a veteran flight attendant and business owner on a mission to help people live their best lives with organic, superfood nutrition. She is an activist for the Million Mom Movement and Real Food Movement which empowers moms (and dads) to be role models for their families by voting with their buying dollars to reject GMOs, artificial ingredients, trans fats and over-processed foods. When she's not flying the friendly skies, she's hiking or cooking with her Ohana!

*"I use Snapchat to creatively share my authentic self, and, in doing so, I've made so many awesome friendships with people from all over the world! I Snap about my home life in Hawaii, my travels as a flight attendant, and my plant-based healthy lifestyle business. I'm about good vibes and positivity!"*

## Marketing:

- Katie Lance **@katielance1**: Katie is a national speaker on all things social media and author of *#GetSocialSmart: How to Hone Your Social Media Strategy*. She speaks to over 100,000 people a year about using the power of social media to build a business that you love. Her focus is real estate, small business and entrepreneurs and this talented #bosslady walks the walk! As an entrepreneur herself, Katie shares her processes for building a thriving business in between wine tastings and her kids' baseball games!

*"I love the creativity and fun with Snapchat! When I first started using Snapchat I love letting go of the idea that "everything had to be perfect" and really started to have fun with the filters, colors and emojis. To me, Snapchat is such a fun way to let down your hair and "let the true you" shine through!"*

- Meagan Williams **@megslv**: Meagan is a powerhouse Social Selling expert focused on building an empire by using social networks for sales. A certified holistic health coach and medical business consultant, Meagan brings her social savvy techniques to the public teaching through Snapchat and live streaming. She runs an international team of sales women who are building an empire one sale at a time!

*"Snapchat is a Return on Intention – I had one intention when I hopped on Snapchat: to build a community. I hit the jackpot because that community turned into real friendships."*

- Lorri Ratzlaff **@lorriratzlaff**: Lorri is a social media strategist and co-author of the book *No Experience Necessary: Social Media for the Boomers, Gen X-Ers and the Over 50 Entrepreneur.* She is passionate about educating groups of entrepreneurs and business owners on the latest social media marketing strategies and tactics so that they can build brand awareness, become knowledgeable on how to engage their fans and ultimately increase sales by "Making Sense of Social Media." When she's not creating content, she's obsessed with watching hockey (but isn't every Canadian?).

*"I love Snapchat for so many reasons. Of course, the main one is because of the community and how we are able to build a real authentic genuine community of friends and like-minded people. There's something really special about those who have stayed with Snapchat all these years. We are the OG! We are the ones who see the value in it and I truly believe that just being yourself and sharing your stories will help you win!"*

- Emilia Pena **@catayap**: Known as "Emi, originally from LA, Snapping from Miami," this inspiring woman is a media professional with over 10 years of experience in the commercialization of Digital and Television properties for the US Hispanic and Latin American media companies. She shares tips on influencer marketing as well as her thoughts about life on her channel. When not working, "Emicat" is capturing the beauty and culture of her Miami neighborhood with Snapchat.

*"I love Snapchat to the point that it has become my go to app. It has replaced most of my social media apps. It is television in your pocket. Snapchat allows you to enter into peoples' homes, it gives you an intimate glimpse into their lives, and is a quick and easy way for me to share and see what is going on in the world in real time. It never became more real as when hurricane Irma hit, I boarded and left my home. SnapMap was the only way I was able to see within 24 hrs how my neighborhood was affected. Not CNN. not The Weather Channel.*

*Communication leads to understanding, and the beauty of it, it all goes away within 24 hrs – who wants to be stuck in the past? It's made me worldly with a snap of my hand."*

- Sarah Stahl **@mrsdstahl**: A Digital Marketing Strategist who uses Snapchat to document the unique challenges that come along with being an entrepreneur. Sarah is passionate about teaching others how to build their brand and market their services the right way – through providing value without expectation. She is a wife (who co-works with her husband), a mother of three and military veteran who quite possibly makes the best pizza in the U.S.

*"In all my years of marketing I've never seen anything like it! Snapchat is an incredible business building platform, not because of platform hype but because of the culture that's been created. Users here not only expect, but seek out authentic associations which inevitably leads to strong bonds. The time investment to develop these bonds are the past, present and future of business innovation and Snapchat has reminded us all of that. We are social beings and as far as social platforms are concerned, Snapchat is currently the only one where we can truly keep business social."*

- Kristy Gillentine **@krisgillentine**: A longtime journalist, Kristy applies her experience in print, broadcasting and newsrooms to her digital storytelling. She is the creator of #ChatSnap, the Twitter Chat all about Snapchat where she has brought thousands of people together to share their opinions and thoughts on Snapchat. Kristy's passion and goal is helping people and brands tell their stories using digital tools and social platforms to expand their reach, increase their impact and grow their community of engaged supporters. She's got a heart as big as Texas!

*"Anytime I need anything- business or personal advice or encouragement, a laugh, or even a good cry – I click on the yellow icon on my home screen. I live on social media, but Snapchat is where I'm most comfortable. It's where I can be myself and share my story – fearlessly. The level of support that I receive from my Snapchat community is unprecedented. That's a big reason why I launched #ChatSnap – the Snapchat Community Twitter Chat: to help others find the kinds of valuable connections, friendships and support that I've found there. It's my go-to homebase on social and it's changed my world for the better."*

- Josh Kotoff **@mrscifiguy**: A Millennial SEO Specialist who uses Snapchat to teach the ranking secrets of YouTube. One of the youngest participants in several SEO internships, Josh is often asked to return as the teacher. Josh is a frequent speaker at university campuses on entrepreneurship and creating your own business. In his past career, he worked as a professional voice actor and does some amazing impressions on his channel.

  *A big "Thank You" to Josh's colleague, Hannah Raya @hammieraya who created this book's cover art!*

  *"I've never experienced a social platform like Snapchat before. As an avid writer and storyteller, I've always been fascinated with people's day to day lives. But what I didn't expect was the amount of relationships formed with people from all over the world. It's the next big step in connectivity and marketing, where your personality is your brand and your life is your stage."*

- Azriel Ratz **@azrielr**: CEO of Ratz Pack Media and a Facebook Ads expert, Azriel educates his audience on the why and how of Facebook ads via Snapchat. After spending over $1 million on Facebook ads, he's about as qualified as they come! Azriel teaches his lessons while he walks the streets of his neighborhood and he also shares some great insights on how parenting a toddler can help you become a better entrepreneur.

  *"Snap Inc. has been working the last five years to create the most innovative camera. Snapchat is the culmination of that exact thing. A camera that jam-packs the best features possible to create engaging, entertaining, and quick content perfect for the social media world. This is why I use Snapchat for almost all of my business videos."*

- Chris McManamy **@chrismcmanamy**: Chris is an IT guru turned Social Media Consultant who has the gift of gab! Chris is focused on reaching his dreams and documents the behind the scenes of a marketing consultancy start up – the good, the bad and the ugly. He's a father and husband, who loves to share what's working in social media via his Facebook live stream show, Simple Social Live. Chris is also quite possibly the biggest WWE fan in the history of time.

*"The best thing you can do is be yourself. Don't try to put on an act or a show. And if you are going in to build something structured, have a plan. But most importantly, if you are going to use the app, just have fun with it. Be relaxed and comfortable. One of the best parts of this app is such amazing levels of engagement. It's the highest levels I have personally experienced anywhere. It is like a second family to me."*

- Amaris Mathews @madbleuz: Amaris is a recent graduate student turned social media lover who has a passion for marketing and public relations. When not working, Amaris is focused on engaging with her community through her #WeGotThisWednesday and #ThankfulThursday segments. She's documented her journey to completing her degree via Snapchat and loves to support her Snap community.

*"I love using Snapchat because it's real, open and honest. There are no hacks and you have to actually be social in the platform in order to meet new people and make new friends. Unlike other social media platforms the engagement isn't superficial. I'm surrounded by people all the time, but my Snapchat community are friends. Snapchat is my escape, it's my diary, it's where I can come and be me and not worry about what other people are going to think.*

## Real Estate:

Since my industry is Real Estate, there were far too many incredible people to include them in this section. I've listed only a small portion of the real estate community below. If you're in this niche and would like to meet some incredible real estate professionals then consider joining the Facebook group called "Snappack Live" to connect with and follow inspirational real estate professionals who are using Snapchat on a regular basis to build their business:

www.facebook.com/groups/snappacklive

Below are the names of the real estate professionals with whom I have met IRL and/or collaborated with on Snapchat content and beyond! Even if you have no interest in this specific industry, the below people are awesome Snapchatters!

- Sonia Figueroa @**soniafigueroare**
- Kala Laos @**kalalaos**
- Michele Bellisari @**bmeesh**
- Marianne Bornhoft @**spokanehouse**
- Kim Boda @**kim.boda**
- Michael Meier @**michaelmeiernyc**
- Michael Mersola @**mmjr248**
- Sue Benson @**suebensonremax**
- Alex Wang @**helloalexwang**
- Neil Mathweg @**neilmathweg**
- Annette Portalatin @**annie.kwrealtor**
- Leslie Wright @**leslieiswright**
- Betty Lee @**the_bettylee**
- Erin Anderson @**erinanderson35**
- Sarah Lapsley Martin @**ccproperties**
- Will Friedner @**willfriedner**
- Salvatore Friscia @**sjfriscia**
- Rich Hopen @**rhopen**
- Cindi Reisenbigler @**fab_rltr**

# Resources

- "She's talking" quote: https://www.wired.com/2016/11/snaps-spectacles-beginning-camera-first-future/

**Introduction:**

- Gary Vaynerchuk quote #1: https://www.garyvaynerchuk.com/every-company-is-a-media-company/
- Gary Vaynerchuk quote #2: http://www.businessinsider.com/why-snapchat-is-the-best-marketing-tool-you-can-use-right-now-2013-12
- (1) Seth Godin quote "Talker's Block": http://sethgodin.typepad.com/seths_blog/2011/09/talkers-block.html
- (2) Why Gary Vaynerchuk likes Snapchat: https://www.youtube.com/watch?v=4wdWN_0Bz58&t=154s and https://www.youtube.com/watch?v=jeoKtdCcZvo
  - o Gary V: Why You Need to Pay Attention to Snapchat: https://www.garyvaynerchuk.com/the-snapchat-ghost-is-growing-up-why-you-need-to-pay-attention-to-snapchat/
  - o Gary V: Become a Media Company: https://www.garyvaynerchuk.com/every-company-is-a-media-company/ and https://www.youtube.com/watch?v=rx8m-nYRaGk
  - o Interview of Gary Vaynerchuk discussing Snapchat: https://www.youtube.com/watch?v=f8su93a72YE&t=522s
  - o Gary V: Document, Don't Create: https://www.garyvaynerchuk.com/creating-content-that-builds-your-personal-brand/

**Part One: Snapchat Disrupts**
The Disruptive Forces of Snapchat

- Original Fortune 500 companies gone: http://www.aei.org/publication/fortune-500-firms-in-1955-vs-2014-89-are-gone-and-were-all-better-off-because-of-that-dynamic-creative-destruction/

- [3] *Velocity: The Seven New Laws for a World Gone Digital*: http://velocitylaws.com/
- [4] Picaboo draft press release Reggie Brown "peeks not keeps": https://www.forbes.com/sites/jjcolao/2014/01/06/the-inside-story-of-snapchat-the-worlds-hottest-app-or-a-3-billion-disappearing-act/2/#46c275a2d017
  and
  https://www.google.com/url?sa=i&rct=j&q=&esrc=s&source=images&cd=&cad=rja&uact=8&ved=0ahUKEwjIna7L4qfWAhUP7mMKHdsYCxcQjRwIBw&url=http%3A%2F%2Fvalleywag.gawker.com%2Fsnapchat-first-marketed-as-a-sorority-girl-toy-1113311556&psig=AFQjCNHuGoV9RQxHQeuWoiL6AVYSA0WKfQ&ust=1505584799895829
- [5] Seth Godin Ridiculous is the New Remarkable: http://sethgodin.typepad.com/seths_blog/2012/12/ridiculous-is-the-new-remarkable.html
- [6] Stats:
  o Airbnb Valuation: https://www.cnbc.com/2017/03/09/airbnb-closes-1-billion-round-31-billion-valuation-profitable.html
  o Uber Valuation: http://blog.wallstreetsurvivor.com/2017/07/17/uber-road-69-billion-valuation/
  o Amazon Valuation: http://money.cnn.com/2017/07/27/investing/facebook-amazon-500-billion-bezos-zuckerberg/index.html
  o Netflix Valuation: http://money.cnn.com/2017/05/30/investing/netflix-stock-house-of-cards/index.html
  o iPhone Sells: http://www.zdnet.com/article/how-many-iphones-did-apple-sell-every-second-during-the-last-quarter/ and https://www.macrumors.com/2017/08/01/earnings-3q-2017/
- [7] Spiegel's Three C's Business Model: https://www.youtube.com/watch?v=AqPHordzhdw and https://www.recode.

net/2014/1/26/11622726/a-grand-theory-of-snapchat-as-con-structed-by-snapchat

- [8] Facebook's Decline in Original Sharing: https://www.thein-formation.com/facebook-struggles-to-stop-decline-in-original-sharing

- [9] Facebook offers $3 billion to buy Snapchat: http://mashable.com/2014/01/06/snapchat-facebook-acquisition-2/#x576rKVsOiq1

- [10] Instagram CEO, Kevin Systrom on copying Snapchat: https://techcrunch.com/2017/05/16/to-clone-or-not-to-clone/ and http://fortune.com/2017/05/30/instagrams-ceo-snapchat/

## Camera-First Communication

- Spiegel quote: https://www.youtube.com/watch?v=ykGXIQAHLnA

- [11] Snapchat Blog – *The Frame Makes the Photograph*: https://www.snap.com/en-US/news/post/the-frame-makes-the-photograph/

- [12] 8 times as many photos: https://petapixel.com/2015/12/15/there-are-now-8x-more-people-taking-pictures-than-10-years-ago/

- [13] Mylio.com quote: http://mylio.com/true-stories/tech-today/how-many-digital-photos-will-be-taken-2017-repost

- [14] Snapchat Statistics: http://mediakix.com/2016/01/snapchat-statistics-2016-marketers-need-to-know/#gs.aog09_U and https://www.sec.gov/Archives/edgar/data/1564408/000119312517029199/d270216ds1.htm#rom270216_1

- [15] FB daily video views: http://mediakix.com/2016/08/face-book-video-statistics-everyone-needs-know/#gs.yGfvRoc

- [16] YT Daily video views: https://youtube.googleblog.com/

- [17] Mary Meeker's Internet Trends Report 2016: http://www. kpcb.com/blog/2016-internet-trends-report
- [18] Snapchat rebrand quote: https://www.snap.com/en-US/
- [19] Snapchat SEC Filing: https://www.sec.gov/Archives/edgar/ data/1564408/000119312517029199/d270216ds1.htm

Real Time

- [20] MTV Reality TV/ The Real World series: http://www.foxnews. com/opinion/2012/06/03/mtv-real-world-paved-way-for-reality-television-20-years-ago.html and http://www.nytimes. com/1992/07/09/arts/review-television-the-real-world-according-to-mtv.html
- [21] It's Judy's Life Channel: https://www.youtube.com/user/ itsJudysLife
- [22] YouTube "completist" quote: http://adage.com/article/ the-media-guy/youtube-stars-phenomenon/295184/
- [23] YouTube reaches more 18-49yo than TV: http://www. ibtimes.com/youtube-says-it-reaches-more-viewers-18-49-tv-thats-not-whole-story-2365728 and https://www.youtube.com/ yt/press/statistics.html and https://www.brandwatch.com/ blog/36-youtube-stats-2016/
- [24] VidCon: http://vidcon.com/
- [25] Kevin Kelley, Futurist and Author: http://kk.org/ Quote: from his book: *The Inevitable: Understanding the Twelve Technological Forces That Will Shape Our Future*
- [26] Spiegel's Instant Expression Quote:https://www.recode. net/2015/6/8/11563322/snapchat-ceo-evan-spiegel-on-diversity-features-for-the-olds-and-more and Spiegel discusses Snapchat: https://www.bizjournals.com/sanjose/news/ 2014/01/27/evan-spiegel-preaches-the-true-meaning .html

- [27] Timeline chart BI Intelligence: http://www.businessinsider.com/the-live-streaming-video-report-forecasts-emerging-players-and-key-trends-for-brands-and-publishers-next-big-opportunity-2016-8
- [28] Spiegel's Live and communicate quote: https://www.recode.net/2016/5/9/11594144/evan-spiegel-snapchatandhttps://genius.com/Snapchat-2014-axs-partner-summit-keynote-annotated

## Disappearing Content

- Spiegel Deletion quote: http://www.telegraph.co.uk/technology/social-media/10452668/Snapchats-Evan-Spiegel-Deleting-should-be-the-default.html
- [29] Jurgenson's *"The Liquid Self"*: https://www.snap.com/en-US/news/post/the-liquid-self/
- [30] "Whitewalling": http://www.populatedigital.com/online-privacy/whitewalling-the-new-trend-in-facebook-identity-management/ and Danah Boyd blog http://www.zephoria.org/thoughts/archives/2010/11/08/risk-reduction-strategies-on-facebook.html
- [31] Spiegel quotes about disappearing content: https://thenewinquiry.com/pics-and-it-didnt-happen/ and Recode interview 2014 https://www.recode.net/2014/6/11/11627844/three-la-boys-evan-spiegel-sean-rad-and-michael-heyward

## Vertical Video

- Spiegel quote: http://www.adweek.com/digital/heres-how-snapchats-ceo-plans-conquer-advertising-world-165339/
- [32] Vertical Viewing 94% of the time: http://www.huffingtonpost.com/advertising-week/yes-its-really-time-to-ge_b_12374332.html

- (33) Mobile view time: https://techcrunch.com/2017/03/03/u-s-consumers-now-spend-5-hours-per-day-on-mobile-devices/
- (34) Mary Meeker's Internet Trends Report 2015: http://www.kpcb.com/blog/2015-internet-trends
- (35) YouTube information: https://youtube.googleblog.com/2015/07/youtube-mobile-updates-2015.html, https://www.youtube.com/watch?v=O6JPxCBlBh8 andhttp://www.businessinsider.com/comscore-adds-youtube-mobile-metrics-2017-2?utm_source=feedly&utm_medium=referral
- (36) Instagram information: http://blog.instagram.com/post/127722429412/150827-portrait-and-landscape and https://business.instagram.com/blog/vertical-format-ads
  o Instagram Stories: https://techcrunch.com/2017/04/13/instagram-stories-bigger-than-snapchat/
- (37) Facebook Information: https://www.facebook.com/business/news/upgrading-facebook-video-for-people-and-advertisers https://newsroom.fb.com/news/2017/02/new-ways-to-watch-facebook-video/ http://www.adweek.com/digital/facebook-vertical-video-ads-just-went-live-and-are-producing-great-results-173276/ http://www.latimes.com/business/la-fi-snapchat-vertical-video-20150715-story.html https://www.likeable.com/blog/2017/3/facebook-vertical-video-rollout-continues
- (38) Twitter Information: http://mashable.com/2017/05/04/twitter-moments-ads-snapchat/#p0EPfOvM6aqt
- (39) Snap Ads have 9x higher engagement: https://forbusiness.snapchat.com/
- (40) Adweek.com Snapchat Ad performance: http://www.adweek.com/digital/snapchat-launches-colossal-expansion-its-advertising-ushering-new-era-app-171924/ and 3V Ads: https://techcrunch.com/2015/06/22/dadvertising/ and http://www.adweek.

com/digital/heres-how-snapchats-ceo-plans-conquer-advertising-world-165339/

- [41] Snapchat Persuades Companies to use Vertical Video: http://www.adweek.com/digital/snapchat-persuades-brands-go-vertical-their-video-164305/

Augmented Reality

- Tim Cook Quote: http://www.businessinsider.com/apple-ceo-tim-cook-explains-augmented-reality-2016-10
- [42] Augmented Reality Definition: https://www.merriam-webster.com/dictionary/augmented%20reality
- [43] Snapchat acquires Looksery: https://techcrunch.com/2015/09/15/snapchat-looksery/
- [44] Looksery Kickstarter & Acquisition: https://techcrunch.com/2014/06/04/looksery-launches-on-kickstarter-with-an-app-that-makes-you-look-better-or-just-funnier-on-video-chat/
- [45] Snapchat World Lenses: https://www.theverge.com/2017/4/18/15333130/snapchat-world-Lenses-something-new-for-facebook-to-copy
- [46] Snapchat acquires Cimagine: __https://venturebeat.com/2016/12/24/snap-reportedly-acquired-augmented-reality-startup-cimagine-media-for-up-to-40-million/
- [47] Snapchat Lenses 16 Million views: https://blog.hootsuite.com/snapchat-statistics-for-business/
- [48] Snapchat Lens Quote: https://storage.googleapis.com/snapchat-web/success-stories/pdf/overview/pdf_sponsored_Lenses_overview_en.pdf
- [49] Snapchat advertisers purchase Lenses: http://www.adweek.com/digital/why-advertisers-are-forking-over-big-bucks-custom-snapchat-Lenses-172417/ and http://www.businessinsider.com/advertisers-absolutely-love-snapchats-most-premium-ad-format-and-that-ought-to-worry-its-rivals-2016-5

- [50] Taco Bell: http://www.adweek.com/digital/taco-bells-cinco-de-mayo-snapchat-Lens-was-viewed-224-million-times-171390/
- [51] X-Men https://storage.googleapis.com/snapchat-web/success-stories/pdf/pdf_xmen_en.pdf
- [52] Snapchat Geofilters Success Stories: https://forbusiness.snapchat.com/success-stories
- [53] Snapchat hires AR specialists: http://www.businessinsider.com/snapchat-hires-raffael-dickreuter-as-augmented-reality-designer-2016-7 and https://www.fastcompany.com/3052209/vr-and-augmented-reality-will-soon-be-worth-150-billion-here-are-the-major-pla
- [54] Spectacle Patents: https://www.cbinsights.com/blog/snapchat-patents/ and https://www.sec.gov/Archives/edgar/data/1564408/000119312517029199/d270216ds1.htm

**Part Two: Snapchat's Psychology**
An Irresistible App

- Nir Eyal Quote: *Hooked: How to Build Habit-Forming Products*
- [55] Snapchat is most downloaded app: http://mashable.com/2016/12/06/most-downloaded-apps-2016/
- [56] Snapchat growth: http://www.adweek.com/digital/snapchat-is-the-fastest-growing-social-network-infographic/

Creatures of Habit

- [57] 35,000 decisions per day: https://go.roberts.edu/leadingedge/the-great-choices-of-strategic-leaders
- [58] Reward Molecule: https://www.psychologytoday.com/blog/the-athletes-way/201211/the-neurochemicals-happiness

Hooked

- [59] Nir Eyal, *Hooked: How to Build Habit-Forming Products & NirandFar.com:*
  https://www.nirandfar.com/hooked
  https://www.nirandfar.com/2015/04/psychology-of-snapchat.html
  https://www.nirandfar.com/2012/03/want-to-hook-your-users-drive-them-crazy.html
  Habit forming devices by design: https://www.nytimes.com/2015/12/06/technology/personaltech/cant-put-down-your-device-thats-by-design.html?mcubz=0
- [60] Unprompted User Engagement: https://www.nirandfar.com/2013/12/hunting-for-habits-keying-in-on-smart-design-to-make-a-product-irresistible.html

FOMO Sells Spectacles Sidebar

- [61] Snapbots: https://www.spectacles.com/snapbot/
- [62] Sunk Cost Fallacy: https://youarenotsosmart.com/2011/03/25/the-sunk-cost-fallacy/

The Psychology of Snapchat

- [63] Quote: *The Social Organism: A Radical Understanding of Social Media to Transform Your Business and Life*: https://www.hachettebookgroup.com/titles/michael-j-casey/the-social-organism/9780316359542/

Tribes

- [64] Maslow's hierarchy of needs: https://www.simplypsychology.org/maslow.html

- [65] Seth Godin's Book: *Tribes: We Need You to Lead Us*
- [66] Jeff Goins Blog Article on Tribes -*3 Truths About Tribes & Why We Need Them:* https://goinswriter.com/need-tribes/
- [67] Nathan Jurgenson Snapchat Sociologist: https://www.buzzfeed.com/jwherrman/meet-the-unlikely-academic-behind-snapchats-new-pitch?utm_term=.aiZVqGZY69#.rkzrlYvmgK
  - Jurgenson & Spiegel Binary Concept Static Profile: https://www.snap.com/en-US/news/page/5/
  - https://www.snap.com/en-US/news/page/5/
  - https://www.snap.com/en-US/news/page/6/
- Messaging Behaviors:
  - [68]Smartphone ownership: https://wearesocial.com/special-reports/digital-in-2017-global-overview
  - [69] Phantom Vibration Syndrome: https://www.cbsnews.com/news/phantom-vibration-syndrome-common-in-cell-phone-users/
  - [70] Texts per day: http://pewinternet.org/Reports/2011/Cell-Phone-Texting-2011/Main-Report/How-Americans-Use-Text-Messaging.aspx
  - [71] 50% time spent in mobile apps: https://marketingland.com/report-50-digital-media-time-now-spent-within-five-mobile-apps-222543
  - [72] Using Messaging apps more than social: http://www.economist.com/news/business-and-finance/21696477-market-apps-maturing-now-one-text-based-services-or-chatbots-looks-poised?fsrc=rss

Facial Recognition

- [73] Brain Fusiform: http://www.huffingtonpost.com/2012/10/24/facial-recognition-brain-fusiform-gyrus_n_2010192.html

- (74) 30% of brain is reserved only for visual processing: http:// discovermagazine.com/1993/jun/thevisionthingma227
- (75) 50% of brain used for visual processing: http://neomam. com/interactive/13reasons/
- (76) Babies and faces: http://theconversation.com/face-time- heres-how-infants-learn-from-facial-expressions-53327 and https://www.ncbi.nlm.nih.gov/pmc/articles/PMC3021497/ and *Social and Personality Development* by David R. Shaffer
- (77) Grandmother brain cells: https://www.newscientist.com/ article/dn7567-why-your-brain-has-a-jennifer-aniston-cell/
- (78) Jennifer Aniston brain cells: https://www.nature.com/articles/ nature03687.epdf?referrer_access_token=SJKImQtOrPY0lWUu- hZPketRgN0jAjWel9jnR3ZoTv0OT5GxW2TgiUHZmXETmpiU- nUkcqRaQgND2VvyOMl2Jp7IqPMir0s4LiVdjGb0BWT8_ltEY- 0SUTOfl1M8IogrNEK9hFHgXZkeUizW9Sz_MMhdUfnMbAJIY- t1Had1hQ4JFH_ndU1q1DdarpSnzTYnNIH&tracking_referrer=www. nature.com
  And
  https://qz.com/740481/the-jennifer-aniston-neuron-is-the- foundation-of-compelling-new-memory-research/
- (79) Mirror Neurons: http://cultureofempathy.com/References/ Mirror-Neurons.htm
- (80) Eye contact: https://www.ncbi.nlm.nih.gov/pubmed/26514295 and
  https://www.glamour.com/story/eye-contact-syncs- brain-activity
- (81) Emoji usage: 92% http://www.adweek.com/digital/ report-92-of-online-consumers-use-emoji-infographic/
- (82) 75% use Emojis and we send 96 per day: https://thenextweb. com/insider/2015/06/23/the-psychology-of-emojis/#.tnw_6ZjGS2At
- (83) Emoji Studies: http://www.tandfonline.com/doi/abs/10.108 0/17470919.2013.873737?journalCode=psns20& https://www.emogi.com/#emogi-demo

https://engineering.instagram.com/emojineering-part-1-ma-
chine-learning-for-emoji-trendsmachine-learning-for-emoji-
trends-7f5f9cb979ad#.3f2o44ths)

o [84] Oxford Dictionary word of the year
https://thinkprogress.org/are-emojis-words-science-and-lan-
guage-experts-explain-2d0ab3cda108#.3ndb2cnbv
http://blog.oxforddictionaries.com/press-releases/
announcing-the-oxford-dictionaries-word-of-the-year-2015/
Toys, Games and Creativity

- [85] Spiegel creativity quote: http://www.latimes.com/business/
technology/la-fi-tn-evan-spiegel-bobby-murphy-2017
0302-story.html

Social Media Xanax
Intentional Use

- [86] 60% of Snapchatters create content daily: https://www.sec.
gov/Archives/edgar/data/1564408/000119312517029199/
d270216ds1.htm#rom270216_2

## Part Three: Snapchat Brand Building Formula
Build a Powerful Personal Brand

- [87] Ad Blocking Software stats:
https://reutersinstitute.politics.ox.ac.uk/sites/default/files/
Reuters%20Institute%20Digital%20News%20Report%202015_
Full%20Report.pdf
- [88] Jeff Bezos Brand Quote: http://www.businessinsider.com/
amazon-ceo-jeff-bezos-quotes-2015-7
- [89] CareerBuilder.com research: http://www.careerbuilder.com/
share/aboutus/pressreleasesdetail.aspx?ed=12%2F31%2F201
6&id=pr945&sd=4%2F28%2F2016

- [90] Influencer Marketing and Millennials: https://musefind.com/assets/resources/MuseFind_webinar_cheatsheet.c1fca050cd65cf23.pdf

The Foundation of Your Brand
- [91] Content Marketing Definition: http://contentmarketinginstitute.com/what-is-content-marketing/

Creating Content That Connects

- [92] Gary Vaynerchuk: Digital Mayor: https://www.youtube.com/watch?v=JLh7OBI1lqg and Document, Don't Create: https://www.garyvaynerchuk.com/creating-content-that-builds-your-personal-brand/

Start Snapping

- Tim Hiller Quote: https://www.goodreads.com/quotes/7194163-don-t-compare-your-beginning-to-someone-else-s-middle-or-your

Get Real

- [93] Chewbacca Mom Viral Video: https://www.youtube.com/watch?v=y3yRv5Jg5TI

Get Better

- [94] Snapchat Streaks: https://support.snapchat.com/en-US/a/Snaps-snapstreak
- [95] Story Length: Snaplytics Report: https://snaplytics.io/quarterly-reports

Discoverability Hack

- [96] Snapchat's "Our Story": https://support.snapchat.com/en-US/a/post-live-story

How to Drive Traffic

- [97] Paperclip: https://support.snapchat.com/en-US/a/attach-website

Increase Brand Awareness with Custom Geofilters

- Quote: https://www.garyvaynerchuk.com/how-to-create-and-use-snapchats-new-custom-geofilters/
- [98] Geofilter daily views: https://techcrunch.com/2017/07/15/snapchat-foursquare/

Snap Ads

- Quote: http://www.businessinsider.com/advertisers-on-what-makes-snapchat-different-from-facebook-youtube-insta-gram-2017-2
- [99] Snap Ads: https://forbusiness.snapchat.com/blog/snapchat-ads-prove-attention-quality-beats-view-duration/
- [100] Snap Ads research: https://storage.googleapis.com/snapchat-web/success-stories/pdf/overview/pdf_snap_ads_overview_en.pdf
- [101] Snap Publisher: https://snappublisher.snapchat.com/welcome
- [102] Snap Ad Formats: https://forbusiness.snapchat.com/
- [103] Snap Ads Measurement: https://forbusiness.snapchat.com/measurement
- [104] Snap Ads Audience: https://forbusiness.snapchat.com/audiences

Social Selling

- Seth Price Quote: http://www.sethprice.net/personal-branding-quotes/
- [105] Social Selling definition: https://www.salesforce.com/uk/blog/2016/11/social-sells-the-mini-guide-to-social-selling.html
- [106] Seth Price & Seth Godin Interview: http://craftofmarketing.com/seth-godin/

The Medium is the Message:

- [107] Marshall McLuhan: http://www.telegraph.co.uk/technology/0/marshall-mcluhan-did-predict-internet/

# About The Author

Chelsea lives in Arizona with her husband, Brian, their son, Mason and two Chihuahuas, Sidney and Zeus. With over 17 years spent in the real estate space, Chelsea has been using her expertise in social strategies and digital branding to educate this niche.

*"My niche is teaching real estate professionals to build an authentic and relevant brand through social media and digital marketing.*

*I help people design a clear core message that speaks to their ideal audience and help them develop camera-first marketing strategies that satisfy today's consumer demands.*

*Daily, I work with real estate professionals who are overwhelmed by social media and don't know where to begin their digital branding strategy. I work with the industry's top real estate data providers, marketing agencies and tech resources to develop education and programs that will help them create an abundance of targeted leads which means real business for them and dollars to their bottom line.*

*As a national speaker, I share how camera first platforms like Snapchat and live video are critical to reaching modern consumers, how to communicate authentically and storytell not storysell."*

Contact Chelsea at Chelsea@Talkinginpicturesbook.com or www.TalkingInPicturesBook.com

Connect with Chelsea here:

- Snapchat: Chelsea.Peitz
- Facebook: Chelsea Peitz https://www.facebook.com/chelseapeitz1
- Instagram: Chelsea.Peitz
- Twitter: @ChelseaPeitz
- LinkedIn: Chelsea Peitz https://www.linkedin.com/in/chelseapeitz/

Made in the USA
San Bernardino, CA
31 October 2018